My Obsession 4 God

If You Could Feel What I Touch

Reverend Davie l. Woodard

iUniverse, Inc.

New York   Bloomington

MY OBSESSION 4 GOD
If You Could Feel What I Touch

iUniverse books may be ordered through booksellers or by contacting:

iUniverse
1663 Liberty Drive
Bloomington, IN 47403
www.iuniverse.com
1-800-Authors (1-800-288-4677)

ISBN: 978-1-4401-1381-9 (sc)
ISBN: 978-1-4401-1382-6 (ebook)

Printed in the United States of America

Library of Congress Control Number: 2009930721

iUniverse rev. date: 8/20/2010

Book Summary

First of all and foremost I do not apologize but do humble myself with humility to all that read this book and find it offensive or to provocative, though I will not try to excuse myself for much of the derogatory language used and the detailed graphics of certain dialogs describing the events leading up to many unlawful instances, this book was not written to be criticized by any church religious organization or Atheist, nor was it to be taken lightly as to the significance how degrading as to the explicit sexual over tones and the deceptive ungodly transgressions and fornications of the sinful acts of breaking every last one of the ten commandments. Yet I am still alive and walking and talking the word of God, take heed less you judge that which was meant to be enlightened that it may deter others from falling prey to the weakness of the flesh, I hid nothing from ones ideology in hopes that after reading about the life I lived they would be wiser and have more knowledge than I did and not follow the same path as I surcame to which left many shattered lives by the way side through my ignorance. But God be the glory for in him did

I find the light and came forth out of darkness, where I did begin to see, and was able to hear the word of the only true wise God. And now in him I move, in him I have my being and in him I live, so be you not hypercritical of me for sharing my life and betraying it in the only possible way I could and that was by telling the story like it really happened, and pray that all that read it can except my life as a good and faithful servant for the love and glory of God now and forever more. If there be any contemplating that are aroused and raised their voices against me, take heed for there is but only one judge and he comes bearing a two edged sword, one side for truth which I have spoken and the other side for evil in which I have repented and been saved, sanctified, filled with the holy spirit, and born again.

This book is for people that have compassion and love for their brothering regardless of circumstances surrounding the magnitude instability in which they function in their everyday lives for there are many who stand in judgment of them that can be signaled out from the mist. As it were I was unjustly informed at one time in my life by a prominent doctor that I would find a closely related similarity in my behavior by reading the book entitled. The Little Boy Who Couldn`t Stop Washing his Hands. In all honesty I had an important contradiction +being relevant to all the people that were diagnosed with OCD were exceptionally dedicated to God and had very strong spiritual guidance and believers in the word. The book demonstrated that there was actually nothing dangerously wrong or a threat to any ones well being, instead it acknowledges how caring they were about the health and safety of others by their little so called rituals, such as the washing of hands, or those that constantly clean their homes or wash their windows over and over. Then there are those that use numbers for their creativity, and then there's some that drive a car and may experience an uneasy feeling after running over an unidentified object in the road and have to return back to the area it occurred in to insure themselves that they had not injured anyone, and then there are ones who must remove every tag off their clothing or wash cloth which can become very uncomfortable or irritable .and there are many who have to check their doors over and over repeatedly as a sense of safety and protection from harm. So it is a plain and simple wrong analogist to even insinuate that there is something wrong in the way these people live their God fearing lives day to day. Now all these conditions have been established down through the years as mental disorders, which affected the mind and a sense of being able to act responsibly and live quote on quote normal life. In fact, there is a horrible stigma that has been connected to various conditions which have allowed doctors under the law to make a medical judgment as to whether a person is fit and capable to coincide with the general population, or whether do they present themselves as a threat to others in society in which they live. They have been known simply because of their different behavior than what is considered to be the norm, to be institutionalize and subjected to barbaric therapeutic treatments to correct their inability to walk, talk, move, and interact with their surroundings and not be secluded and withdrawn, from the harsh unjust diabolical prejudice, bigot sexual oriented permissiveness and in many cases they have had to undergo surgery to become sterile to be predetermined and their faith decided as to whether they should be productive with childbirth and to prevent them from bringing another misfit being into existence. For instance for every act as fornicators, murders, thieves, liars and cheats, adulteress, false idol worshippers, and the less fortunate not by choice but by circumstances which have made them pedophiles, cross-dressers, gays, lesbians, paranoid schizophrenics, psychotics, those with depression, autism, turrets, those with post war syndrome, and post traumatic shock and post partum depression, ADD, bulimia anorexic, eating disorders, the ones infected with herpes, HIV, AIDS and those with malaria, then there's kleptomaniacs, compulsive disorder, witch craft, sooth-seer, devil worshippers, white supremacist, and religious fanatics. And then for every action there is a reaction and that is considered to be the church and the faith and power of prayer i.e. the Catholic Church, Jewish religion, the new aged church, scientology, Unity, Muslims, Islamic, Buddhism, Mormons, Jehovah Witness, Methodist, Apostolic, Lutheran, Seven day Adventist, The Seven Hundred Club, The United Church of Christ, Pentecostal, Sanctified, and Non Denomination which through their belief one can find liberty, freedom, and salvation because God accepts all the people who come unto him. There are many in the church and medical society that will label this book as offensive and derogatory to the very basis of their theological and long term study of the human mind, but I am living testimony to shed doubt on their theory as to a long term permanent effect which they say can only be treated and controlled by therapy and chemical substances. I can strongly stand on the word and conclusively find this to be absolutely and deniably false. And when one has been chosen and called by God the church must recognize without any questionable doubt as to the extent of what manner of contacts whether by signs or wonders in which God will invoke to obtain your attention, to unduly recognize his presence as he communicates with you and instruct you to what measure of peculiar behavior will be accepted and embraced by the religious establishment without being condemned or criticized. For it is written that those that acknowledge and know the Lord, God will be looked upon as a peculiar people.

The Vision

My mind remembers very clearly that precious day in the year of nineteen fifty four.

Something special and yet strange happened in my life. At the time my family and I were living on a street called Watson in the midst of the black bottom in a small three room upstairs flat. It was like any ordinary day but all of a sudden a wonderful thing began to occur the ceiling that was once above me instantly disappeared, and the gates of heaven had opened up for me, at first I was struck with fear but it was only momentarily, then suddenly I was at peace in my mind, body, and soul then there was a thunderous noise from above after that there came a quietness, and as I gazed upward I could see jewels of all kinds and silver and gold abundantly, and falling from the sky was money continuously floating towards me without ceasing I was being showered with much more riches than any one had ever seen in one moment of time through the windows of heaven.

Then a soft voice spoke to me saying all this and much more abundance shall you receive in heaven and on earth, for you are chosen to serve the Lord thy God, and there is much work that awaits you in your season, and for your humble and caring heart, the soft voice said I will bless you for your devotion and obedience for it is written. I was excited and so amazed at what was a complete mystery that was manifesting in my life, but even though I was at a young and tender age I seemed to understand I told my mother and everyone else in the house to get some buckets and to help me gather up these riches, but as it were no one saw nor heard the soft voice, but

I myself was persistent, and continued to tell them to get something to help me gather up all that was being bestowed upon me. My mother thinking that I had become ill with a fever or something else became very worried. So my mother grabbed me up in her arms and rushed me down the street from our house to doctor Hasserman who was the only doctor in our neighborhood. When they got me there the Dr. examined me and could find nothing wrong with me, but he gave me a shot to satisfy my mother's concern. They took me back home and when we entered the riches were gone and the old faded cracked ceiling had returned, but one thing remained with me and that was my peace of mind. Years passed and I continued to remain at peace but in the year of nineteen fifty eight four years after we had moved into a very nice neighborhood and had our own home, I can vividly remember it was just turning dark and I decided to go to the store to buy some candy. As I proceeded to go a strange feeling fell upon me something was pulling me and directing me in a path I did not want to go, because the store was right across the street on the corner from my house, why I did not go to the store right across the street from my house, I couldn't understand. But something was pulling me in the opposite direction to a store around the corner, and I was soon to find out what this thing was that was happening. I remember walking two blocks over and one block down. I went in the store and bought the candy. As I was walking back, I was about to pass this house on the street of Crane and Neal, at that moment all Hell broke loose, I stopped in front of this house for some reason I could move no more. I then felt someone or something's presence around me. Curiosity turned my head toward this house that I was standing in front of and to my horror there in the window pointing at me through a dirty shaggy old curtain was an ugly horrifying finger, I remember it well because it was crooked. Then a voice spoke to me saying you are one of them who believes in the divine glory and power of your almighty God. I was silent I did not answer, It began to speak again saying to me, if you truly believe so much in your God with all your, mind, body and soul and he is in your heart. Then prove your love and obedience to him by walking back and forth four times in front of this house without your feet touching one single line on the pavement. I looked at the sidewalk, in which I was to perform this task, and it was very disastrous for it was extremely full of lines, the walkway was cracked so badly that hundreds of lines ran in every direction, that it seemed such a feat was truly impossible to accomplish, but I had taken the challenge to prove the love I had in my heart for my God. I began to step and my every move had to be precise that I might endure. As I proceeded to move through the tangled trail my motion seemed to turn in to a dancing frenzy. If at anytime my feet would touch a line I would have to begin my ritual all over again. The dance continued so long by me going back and forth until I lost all track of time. Before I realized it hours had passed by and I was completely exhausted when at last I was able to accomplish my dancing ritual over the tedious walkway. At the time I did not know that I was dealing with the dark principalities of evil, and I was unaware of the powers that I had within me to rebuke the demonic spirits. My body and limbs were aching from the ritual I had just performed, and all my mind could think of was how all the time that I was doing the dance a scraggily voice kept taunting me, saying why don't you give up? There's no God because if it were he would have removed all the lines from off the sidewalk and made it easier for you to complete this simple task, since you're doing it to prove how much you love him and are willing to be obedient to him and serve him only. The voice said why suffer and tire yourself so? I said in a loud voice because I have faith and believe in my almighty God. Suddenly the finger vanished and the voice ceased to speak anymore. I began on my way back home knowing my family would be worried about me being absent so long. But as I walked another voice spoke out to me saying I am pleased in you for you have showed Satan your strong devotion to your God and how willing you are to serve him. A light shined on me like no other light I had ever seen before. Then the voice said hear my words for Satan will continue to taunt and tempt you constantly from this moment on, trying to enter into you at any given time that he can catch you and deceive you at a point in your life when he thinks your faith has grown weak. So now is the time when you must study to show your self approved. For Satan will tempt you and do things to try to make you disbelieve in your Lord thy God. But for all the tribulations and suffering you endure remember from this day grace and mercy will I bestow upon you for your obedience. And all the days of your life that you serve me thy God, I will bless you always, for now it begins said the Lord of the most high, but I didn't know exactly what, what was to begin and happen so differently in my life and my reason for being. At the time I was to numb and filled with peace to be afraid. My mind was too shattered with confusion and disillusion to even begin questioning the voice that was speaking with so much power and authority, how could I dare and ask what now begins? My mind screamed why me? Where is my sanity I thought? Have I missed placed it or lost all of my sense of reality? But there was no answer to be heard, there was only a silent feeling of peace and comfort that abided within me. At some particular point and time there had been a door that had been opened and the spirit of the Lord had come upon me and I had become as one with the almighty God. As I began to search my mind for understanding the voice began to speak again, saying you were called before your existence on earth and have been chosen to serve the Lord thy God, with all your heart, mind and soul four all the days of your life. I went home and when I got there the ritual frenzy began again, as I went into the kitchen because the linoleum on the floor had many twelve by twelve squares. So I began the dance trying to step in each square without touching a line I continued to dance in a frenzy for some time until it caught my fathers attention who was sitting in the kitchen reading the news paper, he had become annoyed with my ritual unaware as to what I was enduring as I tried to accomplish my feat, my father said boy what in the world are you carrying on and jumping around so much for?stop it right now he said and go sit your self down somewhere, I became more dedicated and said in my mind I must do it one more time so I continued and by the grace of God this time I succeeded. Growing up I played and did all the things any ordinary youngster would do, but my mind would never stop continuing to focus on the words I had been told so diligently in the past, and I would not allow myself to get caught up into anything that was wrong with my friends I hung out with, such as any mischief to harm or hurt anyone. By the age of eleven the temptations of the devil had attacked my very being and devotion to God, so often that the times were unaccountable, but I held fast to the word of the Lord with the utter most faith and a true everlasting binding love between myself and the heavenly host. It was at that age of eleven when I was over shadowed by the comforter and I became a new being saved and sanctified and filled with the holy ghost, at that moment my entire existence had been changed forever by the grace of God, whom had molded me to perfection with humility and an obsession for the God of man. But this change was not going to go unnoticed or unawares to Satan's deceitful ways, in stead he found the progressing of my maturity as an opportune time to set his snares and approach me in a battle of constant pursuit to infringe me into a way or manner for his trickery, in which he thought to gain absolute control and submission to his evil depredations and for me to become short sighted as someone in darkness who stumbles and falls, losing their stability and accord nation of which direction lies ahead with the path of my deciding factor of my complex perpetual destiny.

Ten years old

As I look back the main abstraction that Satan thought to use to derail my love from my God, was by focusing my attention on the opposite sex which was Gods perfect creation. Though Satan in his demominizing and conning deceitful predestined hatred and mockery against Gods shinning star. He would seek boldly and without hesitation to destroy my innocence and virtuous but clean and pure ways that I only relinquished to my al mighty God, but Satan seeing the maturing development of me as a opportune time for pitting male against female, for his sinful sadistic ungodly behavior he has demonstrated through out time without reservation.

I can remember when I had my first experience of feeling something different about the relationship of boy meets girl. It was in the summer time and I was a nice, tall, slender, young, handsome boy for my age. I had some friends that lived around the corner from me who had a cousin visiting here from Mississippi she had come to stay the summer with them. When I went around the corner to visit my friends, I saw her standing there she was pretty as an angle, I immediately fell in love with her, but as a young boy you are really unaware how to approach someone as likable as her and express your feelings toward them. So when my friends introduced her to me and told me how old she was, from right then her age was to become the name we would call her, even though she was older, we did this just to aggravate her because she really looked younger than her age. That was a very special summer for me and ten year old, we had become very close friends and liked each other very much, at my tender young age I really didn't know anything very much about love, but I knew that the feelings I had for her was something special and different than anything I had ever felt for a girl in my life. Soon the autumn leaves had arrived and summer was coming to an end. And my special friend was preparing to return back to her home down south, and I was beginning to miss her company already, so on the last day before she left I arrived around the corner as I had did everyday that summer and strangely enough she was sitting alone outside on the porch steps, and she was not smiling or trying to chase and hit me like she did so many times before when I called her ten year old. Instead she just remained sitting, looking troubled and sad, I sat down next to her to try and find out what was the matter, or rather what was on her mind. As I looked over at her pretty little face, a tear was tinkling from her eye and down her cheek, I took my finger and wiped it away, but as soon as I had done that another came, so I put my hand on her shoulder and asked her why was she crying? So she looked at me and answered saying I haven't slept all night long thinking about how I was leaving today, I said is that all that this crying is about I said you're not doing anything but going back home and enjoy being with your friends again in Birmingham. Then she turned facing me and held my hand and said yes that's all true, but the part that hurts me the most is that I'll be leaving you my very best friend, then she said in a shy voice, will you be my boy friend and all ways remember me when I'm gone away? At first being a young boy as I was she caught me off guard and I did not immediately reply, so she spoke again and said you do like me don't you? I said yes so once again she said will you be my boy friend, and I replied this time with a definite yes, she then placed her arms around my shoulders and leaned forward and kissed me on the lips, and to this day I have not forgotten that precious moment we had together. Ten year old told me how much she was looking forward to coming back to Detroit so that she could be with me again and she told me how she was going to truly miss me. So while we waited together we laughed and talked until they began loading the car up with her belongings to take her back home to Birmingham. As she entered the car and they began to drive off I watched her pretty little face glaring through the rear window until they were no longer in sight. As I waited and thought of her and all the fun we had and the good times we were going to have on her return next summer. That winter seemed the longest I had ever seen, when it was finally over and spring seemed so near. I had no idea what was about to happen that would have a big impact on my life. At the time I was too young to really be involved with civil rights, let alone to know anything about segregation and how badly the blacks were being treated in the south, by me growing up in the north and especially by me being raised up in Detroit a place known for not taking any no science from the white man. But soon unbeknown to me I was about to have a wide awakening and become educated about racism and discrimination very fast, but this would come about by a shocking, heart aching tragedy. It was murder in the south by some red neck racist that was ignorant to the fact of having change in the south. I first heard of the incident on the news program, but it still didn't have any affect on me when I heard them broadcast that a bomb had exploded in a little southern church in Birmingham, killing four little colored girls, when I saw it on TV and heard my mother and father talking about it, and saying how sad it was that the people would be little them selves and commit such a senseless act, and take the lives of four little children just because of their hatred for colored people was a out right cowardly act by some simple minded racist. I listened but it had no immediate impact on me until I went outside to play with my friends, and they asked me had I been around the corner to see my friends yet? And I "said no!!", then they said well I guess you haven't heard the news about ten years old? And "I said no!!' what about her? And they said she had been killed in a church bombing in Birmingham, her death and the church bombing had not connected with the two being related in my head yet. That's when they told me that she was one of the little girls who had died in the bombing of a Birmingham church, my legs became limp and my heart sank to the news, no one knew what I was feeling inside and how empty I felt, I turned away from my friends as not to let them see the tears that were building up inside my eyes. Then I began to walk back to my house and sat out on the porch thinking about ten year old and how she wouldn't be coming back to Detroit this summer or any other summer. I couldn't get her off my mind I began to visualize her and think about her long pony tail, and her pretty green eyes, her smooth skin and her beautiful smile and her happy laugher, and I could almost even smell her sweet scent. I remembered how I would call her ten year old and how she would begin to chase me to try and hit me with her little love tap. Most of all I remembered the last day I talked to her and she asked me to be her boyfriend. But what had stayed with me to this day was the innocent kiss of a ten year old. After a while my mind wondered and I searched for some kind of reasoning for this tragedy that had wounded my heart, so I questioned God and asked him how could this happen to me after you had told me that you'd always be with me and protect me from harm. Yet you did not protect my heart from being hurt, and then God spoke to my mind and "said, your heart you have given to me and it shall heal for I am a God of love and kindness", The devil seeks to destroy and kill, but I allow only what is good for you. For I am a God of life, what you have endured will only prepare and strengthen your heart for all the misery and turmoil that lies ahead. The covenant between us shall not be broken or void, I am God and will be with you away. In spite of all that had happened to ten year old I still did not harness any hatred for the white race, I guess I was just too young and for giving.

Little Burnt White Girl

As school resumed I was all ready and set for a new semester to begin. We had a new girl to come and attend our class and she was a white girl. She had been the victim of a fire and her face and upper part of her body had been badly burned. She was ignored and treated as someone different by all the kids in our class. At first if I was lined up behind her when we went to the water fountain I could not drink behind her for some reason, I could not bear to make myself drink after her so I would just bend over and pretend that I had taken a drink. I never restrained myself always from her, I always spoke to her with a happy hello, and I treated her as any other ordinary individual. Then one day out of the clear blue, while we were in the lunch room eating as we so regularly did everyday. In the past she had always sat alone in the lunch room having her lunch by herself, but this particular day when she went through the meal line and got her lunch tray prepared, when she started walking away for some unknown reason she walked directly to the table I was sitting at, and sat right across the table from me, when she did this the other kids that were sitting at the same table with me got up and took their trays and moved to another table. I myself did not move I remained sitting, at first I could not look her directly in her face, truthfully I lost my appetite and could not finish eating my lunch. The next day she went through the meal line and prepared her tray and then searched the lunch room with her eyes until she had spotted me, this time I was sitting alone at the same table as before. She walked straight over to where I was sitting and put down her tray, and then sat down across from me again as she did before, but this time it was something different about her as she strained her burnt face to smile at me, I smiled back and started going through my little brown bag to see what my mother packed for me to eat that day, as I unwrapped my sandwich I held my head down and began eating it. Then once again the following day she went through the line, this time as she came towards me where I was sitting it seems as though she was in anticipation to get to the table and sit with me. I could see a smile on her face as she approached the table and sat down across from me. This time I felt something strange happening, I don't know if I was feeling sorry for her or feeling the pain she must had felt so many times by being rejected, but for some reason I did not take my eyes off of her as she began to nibble on her lunch. I looked at her and saw her pretty little blue eyes. For some unexplained reason I saw past her burnt skin and saw the beauty of God in her. As I began eating I continued staring at her. I could tell she knew I was looking at her and suddenly she stared back at me in a blushing manner and then she continued to finish her lunch. So as it were each and every day she continued to join me at the same time and at our same table, it was just her and I enjoying our lunch period together. As time would have it gradually we began sharing different deserts with one another, and we started a dialog, laughing and talking about something humorous that might have occurred in school that day. There were many things we found amusing. Then one day I asked her just how did she happen to end up choosing my school to attend? And she answered me with a very startling story, she told me that after the tragic fire accident, she had to remain in the hospital recovering for quite a lengthy time, and when she was finally well enough to return back to school, where she had previously attended she had fell behind a grade. And all of the close class mates that she had once known were no longer students at the school she once loved and enjoyed being there with them. They had all passed and were now in a higher grade attending a different class then she was. That's when I found out that she was a year older then I was, as she continued to talk to me a sudden sadness fell upon her when she told me how terrible and bad she had been treated by the students in her new class, whom she did not know before her accident, they talked about her and teased her until it would bring her to tears each day. And they complained to their parents, saying that she was disgusting and to horrible to look at. So finally under the parents pressure and complaints to the schools principle her parents were advised that the school thought it in the best interest of the students and her self, that they should start considering on transferring her to another school. Somewhere that her appearance wouldn't matter and that she would be excepted and respected, and she would not be degraded and looked down on, and the ideal location in her parents mind that would be absolutely appropriate and solve there problem. Was for them to register her into an all colored school, where she would gain complete respect regardless of her fire accident. She would continue to maintain high esteem with the students because underneath her burnt flesh the stigma of her being a white girl would give her superiority over the mass majority of colored kids. I thought in my mind how such a nice person she was. But what kind of parents did she have that could be thinking and acting out in this manner. It took me back to the racist people that had bombed and killed ten years old. Then she looked at me and said something that soothed my mind and curiosity. She said my family are not racist, they were only doing what they thought would be in my best interest, we really like colored people we don't discriminate against them. We are taught at the church in which we attend that all men are created equal in the eyes of God. So we do what the good book tells us is right in the eyes of God. I hope you can really understand just how I feel about you, because it means a very lot to me about the way you feel. I've been wanting to tell you something for a long time, but I couldn't get up enough nerves to do it, but now for some reason I feel it is the right time, and I'm about to burst from holding this inside me for so long, but I want you to know that I like you a very lot, not just for you always being so nice to me. But it's because of a feeling I have for you that I have never felt for anyone before, I just hope that by me opening up and expressing my deepest secret to you, that It don't in any way affect our on going friendship or push you away from me. I just have to tell you and let you know how much you mean to me, being that we only have a short time left before this semester ends and we'll be going off on our summer vacation. More than likely we'll probably be going in our own separate ways to farther our education. So now is the time, and it's the only right time for me to make my feelings known to you, and I'm hoping deep down inside you, that maybe, just maybe you might feel the same way about me as I do for you. Because I'm about to ask you something that means everything to me, something that no matter where I go or wherever I'm at I could always carry this with me and regardless of any other circumstances that may happen in my life. The reply you give to me will make the life I live as one of the happiest joy a girl could ever have. But first before I ask anything of you, there's something that I have to tell you, it's something that I've really never talked about to anyone except my mother. My mother and I discussed that one day when I become of the right age, that I'm going to go through reconstructive surgery to try to correct my burn injuries. There will be multiple operations of plastic surgeries in an attempt to make me look like any other ordinary person. I'm so hopeful and anxiously looking forward for that day to come. Now after saying all that I had to say, I'm going to ask you something that's been burning my heart for a long time, wait! A minute I think burning was a very bad chose of words. But rather I'm going to ask you something that is so dear to my heart and mean so much to me, and here it goes, will you be my boy friend so that when we go our separate ways I'll always have something to cling on to and always know that I truly have someone who cares about me in spite of the way I look or even the way the future holds for me to look. Suddenly I had a flash back it was like I was reliving something that I had already been through once before in my life. I began to visualize that last and final day which I had spent with ten years old. The question she had asked me, and my reply of yes and the joy it brought us at that moment, and her leaving to return back to her home in the south and my anticipation of waiting for her to return to renew our relationship, and the unfortunate tragic news of her senseless death, and all the unbearable pain and hard ship that I had endured. All I know is that I did not want to go through another painful episode, but still and all at the same time I did not want to be the one to initiate the probability of bringing on hurt and pain which could leave someone I really cared about with a broken heart. As I looked into her pretty blue eyes I could see her anxiously waiting in anticipation for my answer. An answer that could quite undoubtedly relinquish a touch of hope and joy with a renewed outlook at happiness for the future of a young girl whose life for the past few years had been tainted with torment and subjected to cruel and ungodly ridicule by a society who out cast any one and every body that was of a different race or was born by an accidental fate in which was deemed to them as unsightly irregularities. Then there was another answer that I severed for the significant impact of denial and a sense of being unappreciative of a useless being, which could subsequently destroy and shatter the very life of one of God's precious creations. My attention for some unknown reason turned to her appearance as she stood in front of me, I began to observe every inkling of her body. This was something that had never entered in my mind before. I starred down at her little penny loafer shoes she had on, I looked at her little pink ankle socks she was wearing with them being folded down slightly, then I took notice of her scraggly long knee knotted legs and for the first time I saw the original complexion and smoothness of her skin. I had never paid any attention to the fact that her legs had not been damaged by the fire, after seeing this in astonishment I eagerly grasped at her pretty pink and white dress hanging on her long slender body then for some reason my eyes skipped her face and my attention was fixed on her hair which was a kind of blond look and it was very long and bouncy as it hung down past her cheeks for some unknown reason, not one strand of her beautiful hair had been singed by the fire, finally I looked into her pretty blue eyes and her face was glowing with a golden glare and I saw far past her burnt skin and I saw the beauty within and not the content of her skin. As she was beautiful as an angel and I had only one alternative to make my decision on for I knew my feeling for her was beyond just friendship between us, deep down in my heart I knew her to be someone special to me, and I would be someone special to her, so I took her by her hand and I said if you want to you can be my girlfriend and I'll be your boyfriend. She became overwhelmed with joy that the significance of us being in school did not matter what action she was about to demonstrate next, in all her enthusiasm she felt compelled to reassure herself of my answer by innocently sealing our relationship with a kiss. When the other students saw what was taking place between myself and her, some of them oohed and some awwed in disgust as to the notion of how could I kiss someone like her, but it really didn't matter to me how they felt about it, all I knew was that I had someone who was very dear to my heart and that was the only thing at the time that really mattered to me. It was nearing time for the school semester to end, it was just the matter of a few more days and the girl in my life would be going in a separate direction than myself. Finally the last day arrived, for the past few days we really hadn't had a chance to really have a time to talk to one another because of all the preparation we were going through to get ready for our summer vacation party, but at last we were together and able to share a precious moment with one another, we talked and laughed while holding hands, then suddenly there was a quietness that fell upon us as we looked in each others eyes, then she said sadly, with her words breaking as though she could barely speak, she then said I don't know how I'm going to live through a day knowing that I wont be able to see you or talk to you at lunch time or at recess, I just cant imagine a life without you, you were always there for me, anytime I needed someone to comfort me and lift me up, you were always there, and knew exactly the right words to say when I felt down and alone, you were there, right across the table from me at lunch time and you knew how to lift me up and make me laugh, I am really going to miss you so much, but here I want you to have my number so that you can call me this summer, at least that way we wont seem so distance from each other. I didn't say anything, I just let her continue to talk on and on, I always loved hearing her talk and I wanted to make sure I would always remember her voice as she continued she said I'll always be thinking about you every awakening day and I hope that you'll be thinking about me also, I said I would, then almost bringing herself to tears she said in a desperate tone "Please don't ever forget about me, promise me that you won't, please tell me that you won't. I said, I promise you that I'll never forget you and you'll always be somewhere on my mind, and I promise that someday we'll see each other again, I don't know exactly where or when I just know that deep down inside me I can feel it, I know it was by God's grace that we were brought together and It will be by God's grace that we'll see one another again. She then began to search with her eyes as to make sure that there wasn't any teachers near by to see us as she gently leaned forward and kissed me on the lips and smiled, and then she said remember that kiss always and laughingly said that had better hold you until we see each other again. We had our summer vacation party and the school day ended. Her mother picked her up as she had did so many times before, I stood a short distance away from her, as I watched her enter the car, she glanced back at me and waved her hand saying good-bye, I waved back slightly as they drove away, I was sadden, but I also was glad that I had graduated and that it was summer time once again. A couple of weeks went by before I made an attempt to call her because I was very hesitant about calling her. I was afraid how her mother would react if she answered the phone, and a colored boy was on the other end, never the less I called and her mother did answer the phone, at first I thought to hang up, but as she said hello I quickly asked to speak to her daughter she responded by telling me that she wasn't in at the time, could I have her to call you back, I said that's O.K., I'll call back later, thank you and hung up. It was another week that had went by before I attempted to call her again after I had dialed her number a strange voice came on saying sorry this number is no longer in service, I then tried the number again in hopes that I might have dialed the wrong number, but just as before the voice came on saying sorry this number is no longer in service, I was momentarily in disarray, how could this be, how am I going to get in touch with her now I thought then it crossed my mind about a conversation we had and how she was telling me that one night she had over heard her parents talking about how they would be moving sometime in the summer, after she had finished her education for that semester and they would no longer have to live in this district for her to attend any longer. The girl I had cared for so much was gone out of my life and it was hard to except the reality of it that I would never talk to her or see her again, but little did I know that by chance of fate some years from now our paths would cross once again. I went on my way trying not to think about her and just enjoy the summer but it was very hard to do.

Rochelle

Finally one day I was hanging out at Pingree Park our neighborhood play ground. As I began joking and laughing with some of my friends, one of them noticed a bunch of girls sitting together on top of a park picnic table, so they decided to walk over and satisfy their interest. I walked along with them not really caring one way or another about the girls sitting on the table as we approached them, the girls started whispering to one another cracking jokes about the way some of my friends looked, and they continued to amuse themselves with jokes and laughter until my friends had their feelings hurt, seeing that none of the girls were interested in any of them, they hurriedly vacated themselves from the presence of the girls, and found other areas of the park to seek refuge from the girls laughing at them and making them feel embarrassed. I alone was still standing there with the giggliest girls, but after all my friends had left the girls stopped laughing, and then one of the girls asked me what's your name? I looked at her and told her, then her girlfriend sitting on the table right next to her said Rochelle's got a boyfriend, Rochelle got a boyfriend pushing on her in a girlish way, and she told her to stop, but she continued to say it and push her as though she were trying to push her off the table into me. After her friend stopped teasing her, she asked me where I lived. I told her, then she asked me how old was I and what grade was I in? She was a very talkative girl with lots of questions, we continued to talk and laugh until the night time was about to fall on us and both of us knew that our parents wanted us home before the street lights came on, the more we talked and laughed I finally noticed just how pretty she was, she had very long hair, and pretty hazel eyes and her mouth was wide with big white teeth, her skin was red like if she had Indian blood in her. Suddenly I noticed her zipper was down on her blue jeans, so

I teased her and said ohhh I see something she said what are you talking about? I said I see some blue panties and she looked down at her zipper and saw it was down and reached down and pulled it up, and said now, you don't see them no more. I decided to play with her so I reached out and pulled the zipper down again, she said in a blushing manner stop it, and pulled the zipper up again. I reached out laughing and pulled it down again, once again she pulled it up. I continued to repeat this little motion over and over again, until she finally jumped from up off the table and stood in front of me. That's when I saw how long and shapely she was, she then said looking me in the eyes that I like you, do you have a girlfriend. I said no, she said that's good, then she walked up to me and put her arms around me. I felt her body pressing up against mine and it felt unusually good. She then pressed her lips against my mouth. I was immature in this action, but continued to carry on kissing her pretending to kiss her as though I knew what I was doing. Slobber ran down our chins as we held each other tighter and tighter until I had become aroused. Our tongues sliding and flapping uncontrollably with one to the other and our bodies had started a rhythmic motion with her vagina rubbing frantically in search for the stiff erection of my penis. We were into an intimate frenzy until we ultimately fell to the ground and vigorously remained locked into each others grasp. As she gradually straddled her legs apart allowing my body to sink deeply against her vagina both of us moving rigorously with a burst of intangible heated energy reaching for a stimulation release or satisfaction from an unpredictable childish behavior, that would take us to a level of contentment with neither of us ever having been through a orgasm, our bodies continued to rapidly bang against one another until sweat poured from our flesh as our tiring body's moaned and groaned with admiration for one another, as we untangled ourselves from each others grasp. What ever our organs were seeking from us it would not be achieved that remember able evening; our young tireless bodies had come to know the wonderful feeling of intimacy with the acceptation of an orgasm. We got up from the grass and she told me that she'd better be getting home before her mother gets worried, she only stayed one block from the park so I walked her to her house, then she asked me would I be coming to the park the next day, I said yes I was going to be there, then she said I'm so glad I met you and I look forward to seeing you tomorrow. I didn't want to take a chance and kiss her in front of her house fearing that her parents might be looking out the window, so I just gently touched her on the cheek and said good night, I'll see you tomorrow, I began to walk home trying to really get an understanding in my mind to what had just taken place between us and try to make since of the affect that her soft body had on mine and what mine had on her. I also wondered why I was so dramatically aroused and had a throbbing sensation in my penis. I thought to myself how nice it had felt, and would this type of feeling occur every time we're in each others arms, or was it an accidental mishap, thinking maybe I became hard in the penis because I had to urinate, it was all very complicated and to confusing that night for me to comprehend. All I know is that I found myself twelve years old going on twenty, with my new maturity development allowing the ability to become enhanced with a masculine performance, and that day of us embarking on a level of considerable heated, intriguing passion would just be one of many rendezvous we would encounter. As I continued to walk along to get home I began to approach the neighborhood church, New Liberty Baptist, the church I had attended Sunday school so many Sundays, and also where I had been baptized at. There was an alley way just before you could come in front of the church. I began to walk across the alley just then a strange feeling came upon me, drawing my attention to look down the alley and stop. At first I did not immediately see the tall dark figure that was standing in the alley, then suddenly it was all becoming clear to me, as I focused in on it, my mind told me to run but for some reason I could not move. As it raised its arm up and pointed at me with a horrible looking crooked finger my memory began to take me back too when I was eight years old and had encountered a similar finger like this one that had shown itself to me before, then it began to speak with a scary trembling voice, saying to me as it directed that crooked finger at me. Momentarily, I wondered if I was about to be punished for the act I had just been engaged in at the park. The words coming froth from its mouth were like the words I had heard before when I was eight years old. It said I will give you all that your heart desire if you will come into my fold and give me your soul and become my disciple. I have been keeping a record on you and have considered that you do well to serve me. I have made myself known to you and allowed you to see my configuration. Why would you give your heart and soul to a God you cannot see? I answered boldly because I believe. He then vanished. Like once before in my young life I realized without any doubt that I had been encountered and come face to face with the devil himself. Casually I began to continue to walk toward home, but as I had gotten a few steps in front of the church I began to have an uneasy feeling as if someone or something was lurking in the dark of the night striving to interfere and sway me from completing my journey to get home by their evil lingering presence. Because of the persistence of the uneasy feeling, I turned and went back to the alley and attempted to start walking past the church once again. I had gotten half way past the church and was halted in my steps. I immediately turned around and went back to the alley as I started to walk forward I said God be with me. Just as I had almost past the church I heard the presence in the dark begin to babble something. I couldn't understand, but something didn't feel right in my steps, so I turned and went back to the alley again. Then God spoke to my mind and said go in faith hearing this I rebuked the presence in Jesus name sake as I walked every four steps I rebuked the presence in Jesus name sake, and by the time it took me from the alley to the point of passing the church, was a count of four times I had rebuked it. I had once again done the dance after many years; I danced and was entangled in a ritual between good and evil. I don't know how but I learned long ago without any informative knowledge by scholars of Christianity but by Gods spiritual guidance. I knew I was the power of four and that my every move must be precise. After my altercation and all was said and done I breathed a sigh of relief knowing that no matter what the devil tried to do to make me lose my sanity. I was at peace knowing that God had not abandoned me and that he would always continue to keep the covenant between us that he made with me when I was just a child, it is a true known fact in my mind that the recognition of ones memory can go as far back to before even being conceived in the womb.

It had gotten very late as I rounded the corner to my house. Unfortunately, I ran right into my father who was pulling up in his car after getting off of work. He asked me did I realize what time it was, I said yes, and told him that I was just around the corner. He informed me that he didn't care if I was right in front of the house, and that it was way past time for my behind to be inside the house, then he told me I'd better not let the streetlights catch me again, of course I could not even begin too try and explain about the dance and the ritual that I had just gone through, that was a spiritual relationship that would be kept between myself and God. That night as I laid in bed all sorts of unexplainable occurrences that had implemented in my life with in the past several hours had me seeking an answer or some kind of tangible reasoning as I restlessly fell to sleep. While sleeping I had a dream or some kind of a vision just as Jacob had in the bible. There was a ladder set upon the earth and it reached up to heaven and the angles of God were ascending and descending on it. And god stood above it, and said I am the lord God of Abraham thy father. And this day your name shall be written in Hebrew and you shall be named Chesed. For you shall be of mercy, benignity, magnificent and great powers in your right hand for God. And Chesed shall be the forth name written on the Devine tree of everlasting life.

There will be many years before people would come to know you by your fruit and I would be acknowledged and proclaimed by many as a man of God which I had been anointed by God. I went to the park the next day and met up with Rochelle just as we had agreed to do. When we got together and laughed and talked until the evening had arrived. It had gotten late and everyone had slowly evacuated the park and we were left there alone, we walked over by the parks bath house and remained on the opposite side of the view from her home. Then we embraced one another and began kissing and pressing our body's together moving erratically simultaneously together. This time I told her to unbuckle her pants, as she unloosed them my hands slipped gently inside grabbing hold to her soft buttocks. I rubbed her buttocks up and down and sometimes just grabbing hold to them and squeezing her tightly with tremendous pressure. She would just squirm and continue her movement pressing her vagina against my penis as hard as she could manage. We continued as though we were trying to achieve some type of goal. Our bodies began to sweat, my hands still pressing in side her pants exploring her skin as my hands slide on her buttock. I reach from behind and underneath her buttock and found my hands lying on her vagina. I began to rub it and stroke it rapidly. Suddenly she felt like she had melted in my arms, as I could feel the wetness of her semen coming through her panties. I was continuing to press against her body trying to find me some type of satisfaction, but once again there was none. I knew something had occurred for her and I had taken our relationship to another level. I backed up off of her letting her step away from the bath house wall, and stood there silently as she smiled at me blushingly while she fastened up her pants. Then she said can I have your phone number? As though nothing had just taken place, I told her my number and she told me hers. We started walking toward her home and stopped and kissed several times. Then she said something no other girl had ever said to me. As she looked in my eyes she said I believe I'm in love with you. I did not respond as her little face squinted up looking at me eagerly to answer her back, with a I love you to, there was a part of me that was resistant to giving my heart openly to another girl, seeing that my heart had been broken in my life and saddened twice by untimely circumstances that had accrued in my life. I just looked at her and said very abruptly I'll see you tomorrow. That was just the beginning of many telephone conversations with us setting up a time when we could meet at our private location, it was an on going relationship that had enslaved both of us with a lustful desire that had us putting family and friends aside, while we took time to journey and make our anticipated rendezvous, where we would share a delightful fling and sensation as we embraced one another each time with much more intensity. This fling turned into a venture that ultimately became a task to continue with the momentum to relentlessly see one another through rain or snow.

Miniature Hoe

I had now reached the age of fourteen and I was a slender handsome young man. One day while I was putting a tire back on my fathers car after he had changed the brake shoes, he had asked me to do this for him giving me a responsible but simple job to do, he was demonstrating his trust in my ability to do this minor task for him, suddenly I was approached by a young girl, as I was sitting on the ground lifting the tire up on to the car, she stopped as she was walking down the street. I was concentrating on the job at hand, and hadn't noticed her as she stopped directly behind me, all I know is I heard a voice, say hey boy what are you doing? After I had gotten the tire up on the car I turned my head and told her that I was replacing the brakes. I looked at her again as I continued to put the bolts on the wheel. I realized that she was someone new around the neighborhood and looked kind of cute. She then said you don't know how to put brakes on that car, challenging me in my answer. I said you don't know what you're talking about. My father taught me and I've changed brakes plenty of times before. Still questioning my ability to do a job like that she said your daddy probably let you put the wheel back on for him. She really didn't know exactly how right she was in her speculation, but I continued to exaggerate telling her I can work on almost any part of a car. For some reason she left that subject alone, and said what's your name? I told her, and she said my name is Dolores I just moved over here, I said where do you stay? She said I stay on Holcomb, which was the next block over. She squatted down and continued to talk to me until I had completed the job of putting the tire back on the car. Then I began picking up the tools that was scattered around me so that I could put them away. Then I raised up from off the ground, and she looked at me in awed with her eyes big and mouth hanging open, as she saw me begin to stand, she said in a fascinating manner you're tall, I

didn't know you were that tall she said. As I walked to the rear
of the car to put the tools in the trunk, I could tell her eyes
were fixed on me and following my every move, as we started
toward her place around the corner she began to talk as she
walked switching her behind, she said I've been hearing a lot
of things about you, I said yea' then she said I heard that you
come from a family with a reputation, and that your family
is known not too take any stuff from anybody, I said yea' you
heard right, I said my brother is second in command of the
twelve's gang, a gang on the east side of Detroit regarded by
the police department as one of the most notorious gangs in
the city, then I told her that I was the top leader of the junior
twelve's, we continued to walk taking the long way around
the corner, as we came to about the middle of the block, I
said hold up, I'm going to stop here right quick, she said who
lives here? I said this is where moms live. She had no idea
what I was talking about when I said moms, this house just so
happened to be a after hours joint, where everybody that had
a little game about themselves hung out and drank and danced
and had a good time hanging out with the older fellows and
listening to them as they schooled us to what was happening
back in the day. We went up to the door and I just opened it
and walked right in, saying hi to moms and her children.

Glynn

I then asked her had Glynn been around any time today, she
said he had been there earlier, Glynn was my tightest friend
who I had grown up with, after hearing what she had to say, I
said if he comes back tell him I went around the corner and

would see him when I come back this way later. When we left out the door she said how long have you been going to that house? I said a long time, and then she said who is Glynn ? I said Glynn is my closets friend, he's my mellow man, him and I have come up through the ranks of hard times with each other, we smoked, drank and get down in fights together. We have earned reputations together that we're close like brothers, and if you mess with one you've got to deal with the other. Back in the day he was one of those kids growing up without any parents at his home. He had to look after himself and raise his sisters and brothers on his own. His mother would be gone for days at a time, all her and her sisters cared about was engaging in bowling tournaments and they barely had food to eat or clothes to put on there backs. So my mother always was able to supply them with a good meal on occasions and, I would give Glynn clothes from my own wardrobe so that he had clothes to wear and kept up with the styles that were in at the time. While I was talking she looked through the backyard of the house we had just left and said I can see my house from here it's right across the ally from here, so I said we will just cut through the yard and go to your place. When we got there I saw some guys I knew from the neighborhood hanging around all outside on the porch, as we entered the home I noticed how junkie and unkempt the inside of the house was. Then an older man who I found out later owned the house came out the kitchen staggering with a bottle of wine in his hand, and I glanced my eyes around the house and I looked in the living room and noticed a large black shapely women stretched out with her legs wide open with out any underwear on, and her breast were dangling out from under her blouse. I could tell she was a stone alcoholic and she had been drinking to the point of it knocking her unconscious. And Dolores just acted like there was nothing unusual or any thing was inappropriate in there behavior. I just continued looking around to find a clean place for myself and her to sit, after examing the space she had selected for us to get comfortable I spotted a few roaches crawling on its surface so I took some newspaper and swiped them away before I relaxed myself next to her, where she was anxiously awaiting for me to sit next to her. After we were sitting, before I could begin to question her as to the whereabouts she came from, and how she ended staying here in this dump. She quickly threw her legs across me, I stared at her and said you don't waste anytime do you? Then she said do you like my legs? I then gently began to rub her legs up too her thigh, as I proceeded to question her. First I asked who the lady was laying on the couch that was drunk. She said she's the daughter of the man you saw in the kitchen she stays here with him and her kids. Just as she said that another guy about in his late twenties came in with a bag of liquor in his hand and he was also drunk I asked her who is he? She said that's the lady that's on the couch childrens daddy, I said oh! Then I continued asking her how long had she been living with them, she just said I come and stay with them off and on when ever I feel like it, then I asked her where was her home with her immediate family? She said my mothers house is on Van Dyke and Mack, I said you don't live to far from here, and then I said exactly why are you staying here? You're not related to them in anyway are you? She said no, I'm not related to them the lady is just a good friend of mine, she lets me come and shack up with her any time I decide to run away from home, and I can come here and do anything that I want to do. And then she said I get tired of my mama's rules and curfews, and I really get tired of her trying to drag me and my sisters to church, and her continually walking around the house all day preaching the gospel, and praying for God to save her children. Right away I realized that I was involved with a little run away hussy. We continued to talk and after awhile the drunken lady woke up, I introduced myself to her, and she told me her name was Bessie Mae. She was a gentle warm hearted illiterate country girl. As I laid very uncomfortable leaning back on the couch that Delores and I were occupying. I began to observe at what exactly was so appealing at this household that could possibly draw the constant flow of so many of young immature guys, as we continued to sit and talk Bessie Mae got up and went in the other room where she joined her children's father in some heavy drinking of hard liquor, after indulging for quite sometime they staggered out of the room. He left out the door going on his own way; she went up the stairs and collapsed on the bed. Now it was time for the young guys to make their move, they came in the front door and went straight up the stairs after Bessie Mae. My curiosity got the best of me. And I was determined to see what was taking place up stairs I asked Delores where was the bathroom, she replied it's up stairs to your left, I told her I had to go and use it, so I went up the stairs and started to venture down the hall, as I began to approach the first room I could hear some moaning and groaning going on in the room. I stared directly into the room and to my amazement, there were four young guys on the bed with Bessie Mae as she laid drunken, and they were all over her like ants on chocolate, two of them were lying on the bed and each one of them had one of her breast in there hands, they were rubbing, pulling and kissing on her nipples. Another one was reaching his finger in her rectum, and the fourth one was trying franticly to insert his little penis in her vagina which was an absolute disaster for him, by her being such a large and stacked woman every time he thought he had accomplished his agonizing task of making some type of penetration. Do to her uncoordinated body continually moving erratically in an uncontrollable arousing movement she would buck him off literally almost throwing him to the floor. But he was determined to ride her without any possible intent of giving up. So each time she bucked him off he would climb right back on and this replayed its self over a period of time. I had seen enough of this silly escapade and so I left and went back down stairs. I sat back down next to Delores and acted as if I hadn't seen what was going on up stairs. We began to talk and suddenly she climbed on top of my lap and started kissing on my neck, I grabbed her buttocks and squeezed them tightly, she then attempted to try an push me downward, but I refused her advances and continued to remain sitting up right. She then climbed off of me and grabbed at my pants zipper and tried to pull it down, I pushed her hand away and declined her desire to venture into my pants. All the time I knew what her intentions were, but I had been schooled by the older guys who knew the game. They taught me that the way to have control over your girl was by denying her sexual advances and desires and keeping her wanting you more than you want her, after she realized her attempts were in vain and to no avail, she started to talk with me once again, we sat there and talked until the night was approaching. Abruptly she got up and said she had to go up stairs and that she'd be right back down. I was not prepared for what I was about to see. I watched as Delores came back down the stairs, at first sight I didn't recognize her I thought it was someone else who had occupied the disarranged household, as she got farther down the stairs I began to stare at her in disbelief and amazement at the phenomenal transition she had made, she was wearing a women wig and a skimpy tank top and she had on a very short mini skirt, with slip on sparkling sandals on her feet. I looked at her intensively as she approached me shaking her little behind as she walked. I said what's up. She just said to me in a voice of confidence as though she was assured of herself as to what she was about to do, lets go she said, I said O.K. as if I knew what I was about to partake in, as we went out the door and began to walk toward Mack Ave. I had no idea what activity we were getting ready to participate in. I just continued to walk with her, neither one of us was saying a word. I thought to myself what could she possibly want to go on Mack for dressed the way she was. Then it hit me, Mack was known for thugs, hoodlums, pimps, and prostitutes, and right now this very moment in my life I was taking on the responsibility of being her pimp and she was my hoe. As we got closer to the stroll that is what Mack was called by the Makers and Shakers, I passed a few of people older than I was but knew me by the reputation of my older brother, and as I passed by them they would make a remark after observing my little miniature hoe "go head on my man, or look out baby boy, or you've got the best hand" they would chant, as we got closer to Mack I stuck my chest out and my walk changed to a stride with confidence. I was about to emerge into the big time and I literally had not one inkling of experience to enlighten me as to which manner of statue I should carry myself in to ensure the safety of my little miniature hoe. As we arrived on Mack I glanced down the street at McCullan street which was three blocks down that's where the real action was taking place, you had hoarse of all types.   So many different colors, shapes, and sizes, and there sitting inside their fancy Cadillac cars or standing on the stroll having a conversation among themselves were the real bonified pimps, after observing my choice for the best location to let her begin to solicit, I choose to remain right there on Holcomb, in fear that if we went down on McCullan she might be intimidated or even beaten up by the veteran hoes for coming to solicit in their territory or even a greater thought ceased my mind of the possibility of the well known dressy and flashy pimps attempt to enlist her into their stable and make her one of their hoes. Seeing that she was a young pretty tender fresh chick, who was definitely ready for the plucking by some of those fancy dressing, fast talking old school pimps. I concluded that my best option for the opportunity of my miniature hoe to solicit was right here on Holcomb, in an environment and surrounding that I felt was frequented on a regulated basis by almost every cool dude that lived in the area, just knowing that they were near gave me a sense of relaxation as I watched my miniature hoe step gracefully up to the street curb, she casually placed her hand on her hip with one leg slightly stretched out toward the street to catch the attention of the on going traffic with the majority of the onlookers being tricks who went out slumming and in search of hoarse to fulfill their deluded fantasy for a short time of their lives. As she paraded herself up and down the curb, I remained calmly in charge as I glanced at every car that slowed down or blew their horn to see if she was an available commodity for sale. The enticing meat market, I had no idea how we were going to handle the situation when ever she was finally approached with a proposition by a trick that was feasible. I for some reason took it for granted that this was something that she was familiar with and had some type of experience in it. I was starting to feel a little awkward as I continued leaning against the window with my hand in my pocket clinging to the Slim Jim knife I was carrying. Just about everyone I knew carried a Slim Jim or a gun. Finally, a car slowed down and pulled over to the curb where she was standing. I gradually looked it over to assure myself that it wasn't a policeman in an unmarked car, by the trick being an older aged white man she began to talk to him. I slowly approached the car. My presence alarmed him as he thought she was setting him up for a robbery, she relieved his suspicion when she informed him that I was her pimp and where ever she goes that I go with her, to ensure her safety. He said very quickly get in, we hurriedly entered the car. He then pulled off and began to ask questions, he said to my miniature hoe, you look kind of young to be out here catching tricks, she said don't worry about how old I am, I know I got what it takes to make you satisfied for the right price, then he said are you a virgin? She said you have to find that out for yourself. He casually pulled up in an alley and parked behind a barber shop. He asked her how much for straight sex. I quickly answered in her place and said twenty dollars. Then he said how much do you charge for oral sex. I said very abruptly twenty five dollars. I really had no idea what the going price actually was for these sexual acts. Then he asked how much will you charge for me to watch you two perform sex. I looked at him like what kind of freak have we gotten ourselves holed up with. Then I said angrily "man look here, I am a pimp and I don't perform sex with my hoes for anybody, do you understand where I'm coming from, my man?" Then he anxiously said, I'll give you forty dollars if you have sex with her and have an orgasm and let me stick my tongue in her and lick it out. Then I said very forcefully "didn't I tell you that I didn't have sex with my hoe. I could tell just by looking at him that he was getting excitedly aroused by the sexual conversation we were having. Then he asked me if I could fondle her vagina with my finger while she takes off her panties and let him smell them while we're in the act, I told him alright man, I'll do it, but I'm going to charge you thirty dollars. He agreed immediately anxiously instructing us to get in the back seat so that he would have a ring sized view of her vagina as my finger vigorously penetrated her. She took off her panties and handed them to him as she slipped her mini skirt up giving him a full view of her hairy vagina. I then reached my hand over and started to rub on her as her legs spreaded wider apart, she began to moan. I inserted my finger into her and started rapidly slipping it in and out, he was becoming anxiously aroused watching us and smelling her panties. Suddenly he started making some very unusual sounds, then he gave a big sigh of relief as though he had just relieved an orgasm in his pants. I had received the money before we began our performance, so miniature hoe snatched her panties from his grasp and firmly said to him as we exited his car, you old dirty pervert she said implying to him. We walked back to where she was staying. Neither of us was saying much of anything, almost silent as we were on our route up to Mack. When we got to the house the front porch was full of people ranging in all ages. I told her that I was getting ready to split, she asked me to come around in the backyard with her where we could be to ourselves. We got in the back and she looked at me in a little girly way and said "what we had just did was to show me how much she cared about me and she hopes I still have feelings for her." I said to her you'll always be my little miniature hoe, she laughed and hugged me very tight as if she didn't want to let me go. I backed up from her and told her to go and take that ridiculous looking wig off off her head, then I kissed her and told her that I'd see her latter. So, I cut through the alley and went down to my house and got ready for bed so that I could lie down and dwell on what had taken place that particular unusual day and try to make some kind of sense out of it. I thought to myself, I have thirty dollars for that simple little sex act, and its not that I can't use the money. Seeing how my father had stopped giving me my little five dollars a week for allowance, after he saw me with a pack of cigarettes in my shirt pocket. As I began trying to fall off to sleep, I had an uneasy feeling as if something was tearing at my very heart. I had not realized the consequences of a disobedient nature my life was embarking on, and how I was slowly drifting away from the teachings of God. I found time between spending with Delores to be able to continue making my rendezvous to the park to see Rochelle. The next day I arrived over to the house, of which I called the house of shame, I was greeted by another young girl that I hadn't seen over there in the past few days. Then Delores came down stairs and said this is my sister she had just run away from home and joined me over here. She was a year younger than Delores but she was very much taller than her and was very shapely. I began to have a conversation with her, and Delores immediately interrupted us, and said very sternly to her sister that this one is mine, referring to me, I replied back to her and said you don't control my life or tell me who I can talk to, she said my sister is a hoe and I can't trust her with you at all. Previously on my way around the corner I had encountered a girl bleeding very badly and in agony and crying uncontrollably as she laid on the ground. I knew her and her family from the neighborhood, she was continually wailing and the blood was steady gushing from her nose and mouth. Her mother and sister were trying unsuccessfully to persuade her to get up from off the ground; I knew this girl and some how it had gotten spread around to me by word of mouth that she had a crush on me. I was never really interested in her except as a friend, whom I always noticed that she was a real hot dresser always displaying her cleavage and wearing tight mini skirts, some of them were almost so short that you could see her buttocks, and she had a very nice pair of legs. Eventually after many efforts by her mother and sister trying to get her up and into the house, I said to them, I got her, so I bent over and reached down and put my hands up under her arms, and began telling her to come on baby lets get you off the ground, I lifted her up from the ground and started walking her towards her mother and her mother began walking her to the house, and she thanked me for assisting them. I then went down the street to where Delores was staying I did not mention any thing about the girl whom I had just helped. After we had been talking for a while her sister made a remark to the effect of what had happened to the girl down the street, she said we beat the hell out of that hoe and stumped the mess out of her, and Delores said yea, I fixed that hoe I hit her right in her mouth then I kicked her in her stomach. It finally dawned on me that these two little hussy's were the ones responsible for the attack on the girl who was beaten so badly down the street, but I kept it to myself of what my thoughts were. Delores sat there looking at me as though she was proud of herself for what she had just done, and said to me, that old slut won't be walking around telling people that you and her have something going on together, I said don't you feel bad about hurting that girl the way that you did, she looked at me and said very bluntly that I wish I had killed that stinking hoe, and I'll do the same thing to any other hoe that I find out that they're going around calling them selves your girl. I kept a stern posture about myself and keeping her in check by letting her know that there was nothing weak about me and that she wasn't to do anything unless she got the ok from me and to keep her under my control at all times and let her know that I was in charge.

Another night came and she put on the same shaggy wig that happened to belong to Bessie Mae, and she put on a little tank top and a very short mini skirt, but this time her sister came down dressed almost similar to her, and asked me if it was alright with me for her sister to come along with us to hustle up on Mack, I said that's alright with me as long as she does what I tell her to do. As before we began to walk but this time we had a conversation on the way to Mack, I had to make it strongly stick in their minds that I was the man, and any thing I tell them to do they would not in any way question me. When we got up to Mack both of them went straight to the curb and paraded back and forth for quite a while, then finally a trick pulled over to the curb as he began to talk to them I approached the car and my miniature hoe told the trick that I was her pimp and whatever he say's is what goes, I could tell that the white man was intoxicated, so I quickly decided to rip him off for every thing he had, so I began to talk to him, I said what's the matter? You can't decide which one of these fine hoes you want to choose from. He said hell no they both look damn good, I said well how would you like to have both of them for the price of one, he said hell yea I'd like that. I told them to come on lets get in the car, but this time I gave the directions where I wanted him to drive too and where to park, as we sat in the ally behind the liquor store he began to ask the price for different sexual acts to be performed I told him, don't worry about the price I'm going to look out for you, just hang loose and enjoy yourself. They climbed in the back seat and he started fondling on them, as he became aroused my miniature hoe said let me help you take off your clothes so that we can

47

get busy. They began unbuttoning his shirt, then they loosed his belt and pulled down his pants, when his pants got down to his ankles he said I can't move my legs the way I want to, so my little miniature hoe said I'll help you get undressed, seeing how drunk he was she said let me help you get comfortable so she snatched his pants completely off of him and threw them over the front seat to me, as they kept him occupied I went through his pockets, and took all his money, wallet and keys, then I hollered police and he began to panic, which gave me time to open the door and jump out and open the back door for my girls to jump out with me and we grabbed his pants and began to run down the ally we ran until we were far from his sight and as we passed a garbage dumpster I tossed his pants into it, my girls began to laugh, saying lets see how he's going to explain walking down the street half naked and I know its going to be a lot of trouble when he gets home and he has to explain to his wife why he was arrested half naked. Then we started on our way back home but then we decided to stop by Dot and Etta's and buy a pound of shrimp as we walked we munched on the shrimp back to the house, when we got back we laughed and talked about how ridiculous that drunk white man was going to look when he got stopped by the police walking down the street with no pants on in a all black neighborhood. It was so hilarious that we laughed so much until our sides were hurting. After we calmed down on our humor I began to lean back on the couch and let them have pleasure on my body. We had been seeing each other for almost four months on and off due to the fact that her mother would contact the authorities on her and her sister in order to intervene and seek and find there whereabouts and return them safely back home to her, only to have them turn around after about a week at home listening to there mother fussing at them and praying for them to be saved, after a short time of hearing the same thing over and over again they would take to the streets and eventually arriving back over at Bessie Maes house, and they would continue caring on in the same usual manner that they were so very accustomed to. One day when she was there she had a little attitude with me because she had been there for a few days and had searched for me unsuccessfully. When I finally arrived over there we began playing around as she chased after me to try and get a punch in on me. I was running around a car and laughing at her uneventful efforts to catch me, by coincidence my older brother and some of his fellows were walking by us as she pulled off one of her shoes to try and strike me with it as she repetitiously chased me around the car I sighted my brother and I playfully said help me brother, while she continued in the efforts to capture me her little buttocks was shaking extremely, I then heard my brother or one of his friends say in a sexual overtone whisper, I'll help you all right not suspecting at the time that with all the game and ladies they had, that they were examining my little miniature hoe and taking a very strong interest in her. All the time we had spent alone together I had never had a sexual intercourse with her, I was denying her the very privilege of having a sexual act on my body, which she so badly constantly craved.

Betrayal

The next day as I walked down the ally as I had done on so many occasions to reach my miniature hoes home, I slowly walked threw the back yard to reach the back porch, but for some reason I was feeling a little uneasy, something was going through my mind but I could not recognize the mental stress that was beckoning at me, as I opened the rear door to the house I became more anxious to see my little miniature hoe, but something was not right, there was something unusual happening, I did not receive my usual greeting by her when I entered the house, I knew her sister wasn't there at the time because she had went back home with there mother, but Dolores hadn't informed me that she was going back to stay with there mother, so I was getting a little puzzled, as I got closer to the living room I could see Bessie Mae lying on the couch drunk as usual, then as I passed the wall separating the rooms, to my surprise standing there was my brothers friends chatting among themselves, I said hey what's happening man, and slapped there hands to give them a five as a way of greeting then suddenly I realized this scene wasn't right, there was something wrong with this picture. I didn't want to believe what was crossing my mind, but why were they just standing there at the basement door way, waiting for there turn to hump like a dog in heat. My brain was rattling, wondering where was my brother and why was his friends over at the spot I hung out at, I just didn't want to believe what I was thinking, I had always respected and looked up to my brother as one of the coolest dudes around, and I just couldn't imagine him stooping that low that he'd actually be having sex with her, even if she was just a miniature hoe to me, still and all she was mine and I know he had to have some type of knowledge enough to realize that, but yet and still with out any respect or care about my feelings, he had to be down in the basement with her, because she was nowhere to be found, I asked where's my brother his friends just replied you know how your brother is, he's down in the basement with that little chick. That moment something left me and I had all at once lost that idolizing respect I had for him. I was hurting very deeply not because he was having sex with her, but it was because he was my brother having sex with her, I left out the door immediately not wanting to face him after he finished his betrayal, as I walked down the street thinking to myself I wondered why would he do this to me, and I thought rather or not did Delores know that he was my brother who she was having an intercourse with. I went to my house and I was to upset to have anything to do with her that day. So I waited until the next day to see her, that previous night my brother had come home and he just went about his business as if he had not done anything out of the ordinary. He didn't realize what he had done had played a big impact on my life. The next day when I got to the house I was very cold and hard toward Delores, she just ran around the house as if she didn't have a care in the world, like she hadn't done anything that would make me have a attitude toward her. She asked me trying to conceal her shame, what's the matter with you, why are you coming on me so hostile? I said you try and figure it out for yourself. That night we made our way up to Mack as we had usually done but this time she didn't know that she was out for the taking. It wasn't long before a trick pulled over too the curb, I approached his car as I had always done in the past, I talked to him for a few minutes then I told her to get in, I told him where to drive his car to, where we would arrive to our destination, he turned off the car and immediately handed me the money which I had already agreed to. She had no idea what sexual act I had arranged and agreed on for her to perform, anxiously he pulled out his penis and said come on lil mama lets get busy I don't have all day. She looked at me as in a total surprise she couldn't believe that I had sold her for a blowjob, I said angrily go ahead you act like you've never seen a penis before, get over there and start sucking on it right now, she said I don't want him to bust in my mouth, I said if he does that he'll have to pay me five dollars more, now shut up and suck it. She slowly eased her head down toward his penis as she began to wrap her lips around it she stopped and made a disgusting sound, I said go a head and get threw he's on a ten minute time clock and I don't plan to be here all day, while she was sucking I looked at her with a sense of satisfaction and revenge for her betrayal to me. In my mind this was pay back for her lack of loyalty for me. After she finished we got out of his car and started walking back toward the house, she looked at me as we walked and said I thought you cared about me, why did you make me do something so disgusting, I said in a firm attitude, I once did care for you but you made that all change with one simple decision you made and if you think hard you'll figure it out for yourself. We got to the house I didn't stay to spend time with her as I usually did, I just said I'll be seeing you and walked away thinking to myself did I do the right thing or was I to hard on her and wrong, and out of place with the way I handled the situation by making her engulf a penis in her mouth. But I couldn't worry about it now what's done is done and there's no turning back or any way to change the out come of what had just taken place. That next day when I came around looking for her she had went back to her mother's house. I waited a few days to see if she would return back to the house she frequented, but she hadn't been seen or heard from by anyone. So I decided to walk over to her house and see her and apologize for what I had made her participate, I was walking along down Mack and it was getting dark and suddenly a white on white in white convertible Cadillac blowed at me. I thought to myself this has got to be a real live old school pimp and he was blowing for me to come over to his car, I thought about how maybe he was going to take me under his wing and teach me all the tricks of the trade. I approached the car and he motioned for me to get in, I was anxious and very eager as I jumped in his Cadillac, I started talking about how sharp his Cadillac was and how I was going to have me one some day. I wasn't paying any attention to where he was driving me to, I really didn't care at the time I was to enthused by him and the fancy car. Suddenly I realized he had turned down a dark side street and stopped and turned off the car, I said what are you doing here? Are we waiting for one of your hoes? He replied no we're not. Then he said I want to have oral sex with you, I was startled I thought is this man I admired and thought was a pimp gay, but how could that be he was dressed so sharp like a pimp and had on diamond rings and he talked in a regular voice not feminine, I just couldn't believe that he was a gay person. Then by him seeing me hesitate with my curiosity, he said I'll give you twenty dollars for you to let me have oral sex with you? I said I don't have time as my hand franticly searched in the darkness for the door handle, he said again come on let me just have you for a while, I said again I don't have time I'm on the way to see my girlfriend hoping that might unquench his taste. But it just infuriated him the more, as he suddenly hollered loudly it's not going to take me but a minute to suck your dick, my hand had searched and finally found the door handle I immediately opened the door and ran back toward Mack, where I felt safe from him stalking me, then suddenly he quickly drove by me in anger. Fortunately I was just a block from where Delores lived, I arrived at her door and knocked and a girl answered the door that I had never seen before she let me in, I asked her was Delores there she yelled and said Delores it's somebody here to see you, she came from out of the back room with a big smile on her face when she saw me standing there, she quickly walked over to me and gave me a big hug, we sat down and began talking, I asked her where was her mother? She said she's gone to church praying for our souls to be saved as usual. Then I said who are all these girls and she said these are my sisters, there had to be at least seven of them and one brother, we continued to talk and hug up together on the couch, I then told her I was sorry for asking her to perform oral sex on that man that night and asked her would she accept my apology, she said yes I will accept your apology, don't you know how much I really love you, and have really been missing you theses past few days but I had to stay around the house to watch my sisters for my mama to keep her from freaking out on me. I didn't tell her about the incident I had just encountered, with that gay guy around the corner as not to make myself look like a little punk, I stayed there with her for a couple of hours making sure that I would have left up out of there before her mother returned home by it being rather late. I told her that I'd be looking for her over at Bessie Mae's house. The next day or so, she said I'll see you and I said you can count on that. I then left and walked on my journey to my home. A few days had past and I went over to Bessie Mae's to inquire about her, Bessie Mae told me she had stayed there all night but she had left and had been gone all day long. That's when I found out that she had started frequenting around at moms house the after hours joint, that I had introduced her to, and also in my investigating her movements I found out that she had started hanging out with a girl down the street from where I lived and she had three no good brothers that were nothing but thugs, dope attics, and alcoholics. Night had arrived and I was sitting on my front porch when I heard a lot of commotion going on down at moms house, I got up and walked down the street to see what was going on suddenly I saw my brothers girlfriend hitting and pulling another girl out the front door, it was Delores, my brother's girlfriend had found out about my brother and her having a sexual intercourse. At first I was going to leave well enough alone and except the fact that she was getting what she deserved, then I felt sorry for her as she was continuing to cry out as my brothers girlfriend continued beating her upside her head. She had never had to go up against a real woman like that before in her life but now she was getting her just due. Finally as everyone else stood around just observing I stepped up and intervened and separated them and held on to my brother's girlfriend and told her that you've already beaten her down and that's enough now, so she relaxed and got her composer back and stopped fighting, then while I held my brothers girlfriend I looked at Delores bloody face and told her to get away from here while she had a chance, so she cut through the alley and went over to Bessie Mae's house. She made a big mistake when she started hanging out at moms house because I had known them and been around them long enough to know that moms was a trouble maker and likes to get things started. But this ass whopping Dolores had received would teach her a very important lesson about whom she confides in and who she lets know about her business. I didn't go around the corner to see her until the next day after spending some time with her and trying to stay off the subject of the incident. I left to go take care of some business. The next day I went over Bessie Mae's she was nowhere to be found. She had started to continually hanging out with the girl down the street and her hoodlum brothers who only cared about speeding and hot Roding up and down the street and it was just a matter of time before they would be involved in a fatal accident of some sort with there recklessness. A few days passed then a couple weeks and I had not laid eyes on Delores nor did I know her whereabouts. I knew she had to be having sex with the girls brothers there was no doubt in my mind about that. But that really didn't bother me because I know once a hoe always a hoe, and I had found out long ago that she would lay down with just about anybody so I really wasn't worried or concerned about it. Then for some reason I decided to walk around the corner just to check and see if she had made her way back around there yet. When I approached the porch there was a uneasy silence in the air every one was just sitting out side looking like they had lost there best friend, at the time I didn't realize how true to the word I was, when I went inside and talked to Bessie Mae she informed me that Dolores my little miniature hoe had been killed in an automobile accident while riding with that girls no good for nothing brother it seems he had ran into the basement of a house just down the block, and then he jumped out and ran and left her little lifeless body lying in the car. My heart was heavy laden with pain and sorrow for her and I would miss her dearly I laid in bed all night thinking about her and the things we had done together I just couldn't find sleep for her being implanted so deeply in my mind. I went to her funeral and her mother wailed in such agonizing pain worse than the pain she probably felt when she was birthing her into this world. It seemed as though my life was like a hamster running continuously around on a tread wheel being incapable of coming to a halt, but I strived vigorously in a wheel within a wheel in a spiral distance unequivelent to any equation ever plundered or solved by the greatest of great mathematical geniuses ever born by women, simultaneously I am in the world but not of the world and in God I moved in him I have my being. And in him I live and only through the power of the all mighty omnipotent God coincides the trinity which is the Father the Son and the Holy Ghost and fourth I am through the holy sanctity from the power of the word. But as my heart lingered trying to access the untimely tragic relationships I had encountered in my young life. I turned away from the lust and love which had enlightened me, and had played a tremendous roll in my development of being subject to the tempting flesh and been able to remain abstinent through it all. I had to make a decision and what ever it is I knew I must abide by it. But it was the word of God that was guiding me and it was by his will that I would be instrumental to God and fulfill his covenant. So I restrained my self from worldly things and used my personal strength to remain pure in heart and, abstain from girls and unto God my heart, body and soul. As the vision from God when he had anointed me by the name Chesed, and I remember how God had removed the hedge from around and how the devil would be allowed to do anything in his powers to distract me from doing the works of God, but he can't hurt me or destroy my being because of the mighty power of four that God has bestowed upon me. I emphatically became obsessed with God and I cleansed my mind by being stayed on God and cleansed my heart by being washed in the blood of Christ and continually cleansing my body without ceasing as to be without stain or blemish and never to have a mark on any part of myself that would be a degradation to my partaking in the highest holiest alignment with God through his sacred holy ministry and which he orchestrated to conform me with his reverence. And then God spoke to me saying when Adam sinned he brought on suffering with that sin, and through his sin I also bear his sin and there will always be a suffering that I have to endure. Because God told me he wants the glory and without suffering I can't have the glory for God. And I will go through many trials and tribulations for his glory that I might endure to the end. You can look back at all the misfortunes that accumulated in your past, but you shall not have any inclination In the direction I will take you from, nor shall it be known to you, so you must endure for the glory, because God continually wants your glory. It was as if I had become dormant or in hibernation, I had denounced my action with most of everyone I had known because the words of God had enhanced my ability to deprive myself of many necessities of this world, my daily routine was to go to school and come directly back home and keep to my self. One day while rummaging through our dining room chest drawer, my attention was drawn to an old family bible that was lying underneath a lot of our accumulated keep sakes. I reached down and picked it up and began to browse through it causally, until I had a urge to begin to read it from the very first page, and as I sat on the dining room floor reading one page at a time a compulsion came upon me as though I had a addiction and could not put it down as I craved to absorb every single word. With a passionate desire I continued to read it past my supper time and until the night had arrived and then it was time for me to go to bed and get some sleep. So I could rise in the morning and leave to attend school, I had become obsessed and mesmerized and could hardly contain the anxious anxiety that was miraculously motivating me with an intriguing hunger that I could not contain, the tumultuous degree of spiritual desire and perceptions that awaited me in the holy bible at my home. I was attending one of the most notorious schools in the city of Detroit and it was very hard to abstain my focus on my continuing obsession for God, but due to my brothers reputation of being a hard core thug who was a no nonsense person always ready and able to in gage victoriously in a combat against any rival. I was able to attend school with hardly any incidents of any one wanting to have an altercation with me knowing that if I was misused or abused in any manner by any one there would be a strong retaliation by my brother, who had dropped out of school in the eighth grade but he remained visible around the school as he and his gang of followers he ran with hung out at the park across the street from the school I attended, and that gave me a considerable sigh of relief, but I tried hard not to walk in his footsteps or to depend on him, by his reputation helping to pave the way for me to survive with out any incidents in a place with so much turmoil and ruthlessness. Although I was involved in many fights. I stood strong, and gained my own respect by not even informing my brother, knowing that he would respond drastically. Glynn who had also dropped out in the sixth grade was my main man and I could always depend on him to help me handle any problems that I may have to deal with outside of the school grounds. But there was a bright side to it all for me I would soon be leaving all of that outrages behavior that had taken place in the school and I would be graduating to high school. I knew once I got home and got back into reading the word of God that I would find some kind of conciliation and peace of mind catering to Gods word. But when I had taken it from the chest drawer a certain serenity consumed me as I walked up the stairs to my bedroom and stretched myself across the bed, I began to turn to the page which I had left off on, and suddenly an uncontrollably urge suppressed me, with an obsession to begin reading from the beginning all over again, but this time to be sure I had absorbed and captured every single living word that God had inspired men to write, I was obsessed to read each scripture four time with a needful desire adhere to the consumption of every individual word with out a begrudging heart but with a heart of humble submission and obedience. I had been instilled with the mathematical supremacy coveting me from the principalities of darkness that were presently perusing a personal vendetta against the very fiber of my spiritual emulations to the realm of my heartfelt obsession for my Godly father. I became understandably aware that my most operant and more powerful weapon against the principalities of darkness was the almighty bible and I had to study to show myself approved, that I might acquire and hold fast to the wisdom through my faith and understanding of God's unchanging words. I took to my bible day in and day out to strengthen and safeguard myself from the diabolical treachery advancing of the evil inhabitance of this world, that continually seeks to infiltrate my mind to preliterate my adaptation to serve God in this on going war fare I was embodied in. my obsession four God had an inffluence on the way I thought, the way I breathed , and the perceptions on how I saw things, the way I would feel things as I touched them, it also affected the things I could eat, and my walk and the way I talked. This obsession had control of my every move and with it being within the utter most parts of my body my every move must be precise. In regard to the sacred covenant between myself and God there was but only one way to consul my obsession from the world and mans coning deceitful eyes that were unwavering, and I had to hold fast to my obedience and faith in God. I read the bible four times and did eat every word that I might be full, and enlightened with wisdom, knowledge and understanding. And I walked in the way that God had manifested himself in me. Two years had past and I was now sixteen and pure in heart. This was because of all the time I had spent with God, and I had thought no wrong, said no wrong, neither had I done anything wrong. My brother who was a year older than me had been sent off to prison for his criminal involvement in a string of armed robberies, he was sentenced to serve five years. It was now my sole responsibility to ensure the safety and well being of my family. Along with that obligation came the dominating reputation that my brother had left behind. I was now attending Wilbur Wright High a very prestige's school, it had a Co-op program due to the fact that it was a trade school and once you've reached the eleventh grade you would be placed on a job in reference to the trade you are taking. This allowed you to work two weeks and then go to school two weeks. My trade was tool and die, I decided to get into this field at my fathers persuasion, he was very eager for me to take up this trade, as he had explained to me that there were only a few blacks with this kind of knowledge in the entire auto industries, and plus they make very excellent wages, and also by me going to school two weeks and to work two weeks it made it very easy for me to manipulate every one I knew in the streets. Once again the Devil would sway me to walk against the grain and the word of the Lord. I had an older sister whom

I loved very dearly more than words could describe, every where she went ever since I was knee high to a grass hopper, I was right along with her holding to her skirt tail. She was a very beautiful and intelligent young lady whom I was very attached to and cared for exceedingly. I vowed to protect her from anyone, and anything with all my heart. When my brother went off to prison he left behind one daughter and another child on the way, which turn out to be a boy, which he would never have an opportunity to see or hold because he died at the age of three months, it was a great lost to the entire family because it happened on our mothers birthday. Any way his girl friend whom he had left behind hung out with my sister and they went and did almost everything together, New Years had arrived and I had not yet come out of my hibernation, but to my sisters insistence to get out, she told me that her and my brothers girl friend were going to be attending a New Years party on Mack and McCollum, this was the part of Mack where all the pimps and hoes resided, I was very reluctant at first not to attend, but my sister was very persuasive and told me that I had not been involved with the out side world and that I needed to get out and give my self a break, and enjoy myself for a change, finally I excepted her invitation, and she wrote down the address where they would be participating in bringing in the New Years. I still plundered in my mind as to whether this event was the proper thing for me to attend. I was sixteen and had went to drivers training through my school and obtained my license to drive, my routine was usually being allowed to take my mother grocery shopping or any other places of importance that she had to go. But I did have my own key to the older car my father owned, he had two vehicles, but I was only allowed to drive his older car which was a fifty nine dodge which he would usually drive to work. But seeing that this was New Years Eve my father had a few days off of work for the holiday, and I knew he would not probably object to me using his older car for this celebrated occasion. Earlier that day I had went to the shop and got my hair processed and laid with waves three to the side. And that night I got dressed very dapper in one of the suits that my brother had left behind when he went to prison, he had an assortment of fine clothes to choose from, seeing that he and I were almost the same size. I could fit everything he had left behind in his wardrobe. And once he was gone I could help myself to all of his clothing and also two pair of expensive gator shoes.

The Runt

I would soon become known as one of the sharpest young men who frequented Mack Ave. That New Years Eve night, I went to two party celebrations that I had been invited to, since I had taken my fathers car I was able to cover a lot of territory. Finally after I had enjoyed myself at those two parties, a friend of mine whom I ran across told me of another party which his cousin was holding. I decided to go and enjoy their gathering, seeing that I knew them as well, when I arrived there we partied and danced then a girl I had been talking to from the past on and off entered into the home. She was a very beautiful girl whom I had admired for some time, but I was never really given a chance to romance her as I had wanted. But for some reason she just threw herself at me lustfully I embraced her and she kissed me, her name was Shirley and I had really had a desire to have her ever since I first met her. So, after remaining at the party for a while I told her to come with me so we left and got in the car. I quickly drove down through an alley and stopped, and then I made my advances, before she would have a chance to change her mind. I switched places with her on the front seat and hastily laid her down. I then began to tug at her underclothes. It was a task in itself because she had on a panty girdle. I tried desperately to pull them off of her, as she uncontrollably moved her hot perspiring body in a sexual manner. I was extremely aroused and could not contain myself any longer. I had to have her and I was not going to waste anymore time fighting to relive her of the girdle. I pulled out my penis she grabbed it and placed it between her legs. I just started moving my body back and forth. I tried desperately to place my penis directly in her vagina but it was too complicated with her still wearing the girdle that only rested half way down her thighs. She was extremely hot that it wasn't long before I had an orgasm. As I rose up from her she reached her hand between her legs as though she were examining where my semen had contacted her body. She smiled as though relieved when she realized that I hadn't penetrated anything but her thighs. That's when the reality consumed me with the notion that after all the effort put forth with her, I still had not engaged in an intercourse. I drove back to the party and gave her my coat to throw over her shoulders as it had began to snow, as I escorted her to the bathroom to clean herself I noticed there was one older guy observing us, I speculated in my mind that he had gotten her high off something and had taken advantage of her and had sex with Shirley before I had arrived, because she really wasn't acting rationally. After she came out the bathroom she came directly to me and put her arms around me. I thought to myself that this was all too easy after trying effortlessly for over two years, I kissed her and said I had to go and meet someone, and that I'd be talking to her later. She walked me to the door and watched me as I sped off in my car. Now at last it was time for me to go and meet up with my sister and my brother's girlfriend. I knew exactly where the location of the party was being held, but I had never frequented any properties in that area being that it was on Mack and McCullan a residential territory that I had not yet ventured until that New Years Eve. I was very confident in myself because I knew that I was dressed to the max with a slight pimpest appearance and I carried myself in a manner of dignity and prestige to the point that no one could conclude exactly or approximately how old I really was as I walked into the door of the house where I was to meet up with my sister. I could hear the music blasting as loud as it could possibly be, and at first all kinds of loud conversations were taking place, but as all attention was turned in my direction a quiet calm came about in the house and I was greeted with all types of stares advanced my way. I took a few more steps and stopped and stood in my deviance stance, being checked form head to toe, I wore some very appealing attire and was dazzling, and captivated all the females in the place. Finally my sister graced across the floor to where I was standing and kissed me and wrapped her arms around me, and introduced me to all the onlookers as her brother, then she lead me over to the table where her and my brothers girlfriend were occupying. I asked her who was all these people that were here, never having seen any of them before, she just casually responded, a little bit of everybody, some that just came to celebrate and bring the New Year Eve in. A lot of them are regular patrons that come and hang out here all the time after hours. I said after hours, she said yes, after hours joint frequented by just about anybody in the game of making fast money and have an involvement in the underworld. My entrance had made an impact on some of the females that were there. All at once a furious cat fight erupted between two of the young women attending the New Years celebration, they were clawing at each others flesh and pulling one another's hair out, then one of them picked up a beer bottle and brutally struck the head of the other young lady. Then the fight ensued into a deadly encounter when the one that was struck in the head while bleeding exceedingly, she reached down into her bra between her large breast and whipped out a barbers razor and began swiping at the other girl as she quickly retreated and ran around the table in fear of her life, while the other young woman was enraged with anger as she chased after her friutlessly out of breath, and a large loss of blood, she submitted, and gave up the effortless chase, as she sat down to rest her weary and disillusioned body, the house proprietor called Molly came to her aid trying to administer first aid and desperately trying to contain the rapid flow of blood, after assisting her for about a half an hour she succeeded in her efforts to slow the blood stream as the little women that had struck the devastating blow looked on in admiration of herself as she nonchantely sipped on a fresh bottle of beer. I asked my sister what was that all about? What brought all that confusion on? She replied that they were choosing, I said choosing what? She said they were choosing you with your fine self. They fought and tangled with one another over which one of them would have the option of trying to get with you and become your lady. I said you've got to be kidding? She said I'm not playing with you, I'm as for real as day. You may have to decide on which one of them is worthy to become your lady before you get up out of here tonight. At first I was a little uneasy about the whole idea, then I felt besides myself with a touch of moderation at the notion that they had went through all of that hassle to win my affections. So I carried on partying through the night without so much as talking to neither of them, playing the role as though I had no desire or intentions to submit myself to either one of them. As the party came to a close, and people started to ease up out of there, I talked to my sister to see where her destination was going to be after leaving. She told me her and my brothers girlfriend were going to hang out at her place. I asked her if she needed a lift, she said that they had everything under control and that I could go ahead and leave anytime I was ready. A little after two in the morning I decided I had enjoyed myself enough and raised up to make my move and get out of there seeing that I had to work at my Coop job in the morning. So I left out the door and started walking toward my car, and as I was about to approach it I heard a soft hesitant voice coming from behind me as I turned to look, I could see that it was the little young lady who had been in the scrimmage earlier that night. I said what's up? As she said something that

I was not at all expecting, she said, hey mister can I talk to you, I was very astonished that she had given me authority and proper recognition. I said to her what have you got to talk about? She said I guess you saw me fighting with that over weight hussy, she had the nerves to challenge me over your choice of which one of us you would take into your stable. I realized that I was being chosen by a very experienced hoe. I said what makes you think that I'd be interested in either one of you, she said the moment I saw you come through the door you stole my heart and I just knew I had to have you for my own. I said what have you got to offer me? What can you bring to the table? I knew the right words to say to her to let her know she had to be worth my time and I also knew words to flatter her, seeing that I had read the book Pimp the Story of my Life by Iceberg Slim and knew it by heart. So I said to her I'll tell you what, I'm going to call you my Little Runt, how do you like that? She said if that's what satisfies you. She said mister I just want to make you happy anyway I have to do it. I'll make you more money than you can count and all you have to do is to make me your queen and satisfy me sexually and love me and there's nothing under the sun that I wouldn't do for you. As I looked her over I realized she was a very pretty little thing, someone I'd be proud to associate myself with and become her main man. I looked at her little shapely legs as we stood in the cold talking. I thought to myself that she was my gold mine, and then she asked me if she could hug me. I knew she was dying to have sex with me, but I remembered the pimp's motto to get the money first, then afterwards shower them with gratitude and give them a sexual ecstasy that they'll never forget. So I told her I had business to take care of so I had to be going. She said when will I see you again? Please can I have your phone number to reach you? I said, I won't give you my number but I will be in touch with you when you've got something for me worth my time. Then I said later. I got in my car and drove off leaving her standing there watching me as I sped away, the next day after returning home from my Coop job I was surprised when I received a phone call from my sisters husband. He was calling me from Molly's after hours place in reference to the young lady whom I had met there New Years Eve. He was getting in touch with me at her insistence as she had been anxiously trying to find someone who knew me, and could contact me on her behalf. Finally my sisters husband had arrived there and by her eagerly talking about her acquaintance she had made with me that other night, he quickly told her of his relationship to me and that he would try to reach me for her. I asked him what was up as I began to talk on the phone, he said man you better get over here as soon as you possibly can cause man you've got a little cutie over here about to lose her mind with concern about rather she's ever going to see you again or not. Brother I don't know what you did to this girl but I know one thing and that's about how crazy she is about you and just how bad she wants to see you, and brother I think she's got a little something just for you. I tell you bro you'd better hurry up and make it around here. I said to him let me speak to her, he said hold on a minute, I could barely hear his attempt of him trying to tell her to talk to me on the phone, but his attempt was unsuccessful. He came back to the phone and began to explain to me what had taken place, he said she refused to talk on the phone with me because she was too embarrassed about all the efforts and different ways she had been attempting through the day to find anyone, who might have had any information about a way for them to make any kind of contact with me, so that she could get connected back with me once again, and she also was afraid that I may be angry at her for trying to get excess to my number without my permission, and she was scared that she might have blown her chances of having a relationship with me because of her anxious radical reactions in which she had drastically demonstrated regarding the outlook on our determining factor of involvement. I told him that I'd be around there shortly so I bathed and got dressed in a sharp blue suede and leather walking suit which I had gotten from one of my brother's rap partners, whom had asked me to bring him some fresh clothing down to the county jail when he was going up before the judge for armed robberies along with my brother and in exchange for my clothes he would let me have the ticket to the cleaners where he had a vast variety of designer wear and it would all belong to me seeing he was going to be doing a nice long stretch in prison and therefore he would have no need for them, so along with my brothers clothing and his, I had a very outstanding wardrobe and I was soon to become known as one of the sharpest dudes that walked the stroll Mack. After I had gotten dressed I sprayed myself with some of my fathers fancy cologne, then I began to walk around to Molly's after hours place, when I had gotten there the runt tugged at my arm for me to follow her in the backroom where a bar had been installed, we sat down on a couch next to one another, there she said I've got something for you with a proudness about herself, she reached in her bra and pulled out a wade of money. I tried to stay calm and cool but inside I was very excited as she looked at me and said this is for you baby handing me the money. I casually began to count it as though it really mattered to me exactly how much was there but I went through the motion anyway when I had finished counting, it was a little over three hundred dollars. I had never had three hundred dollars at one time in my life. I gave her a cold stare and said baby is that the best you could do? She said baby I worked my fanny off last night, I thought I did quite well, then I said I think you can do better with your little fine self, trying to sweeten her up a little bit, then I reached over and snatched her to me and said baby you're my queen and its up to you to make me happy and I want you to always remember that, then I pressed my lips up against hers and stuck my tongue down her throat and kissed her forcefully and then I told her that's just a sample of what I have in store for you when you do things to make me happy. I open myself up for you to make you happy to, I put the money in my pocket and for some strange reason I had a compulsion to go to the bathroom and wash my hands. I know what brought the urge on; it was the thought of how filthy the money was. I didn't concern myself at my behavior at the time because I had no idea how infatuating this ritual would become in my life. So I told the runt that I was leaving but I would return shortly and for her to prepare herself for a big surprise before I left she told me that I had to take care of the house lady which was Molly for the use of her room she allowed her and another young lady who she was very fond of to frequent them. So I threw her a few dollars as I was about to leave. When I got home my father had gotten from work, so after I had eaten I left out and took his old fifty nine dodge and drove off first thing I did was to go downtown to a jewelry store and brought a fake cracker jack diamond ring and stuck it down inside my pocket, afterwards I went back to Molly's after hours joint to pick up my little runt, as we drove along she had no idea where we were going. I finally approached a little shopping mall and pulled in and parked. I told the runt to get out and come on, we walked along passing several stores before a store displaying ladies apparel in the window captured my attention, so I decided we would go in and browse around. We had looked at quite a few outfits when suddenly one of them caught my attention. I asked the runt did she like this particular set and she said she thought it looked very nice, so I said tell the sales lady what size you wear and take it and try it on, as she came from out of the dressing room she was dazzling and was wearing it very well considering she was so small. The outfit accented her little curves on her body and I could see she was very shapely. I said do you like it? She said yes. I said that's all I need to know, we'll take it. I told the sales lady and pulled out my wade of money and pilled off the amount for the item we had purchased. The compulsion to wash my hands occurred again, but I would have to delay that ritual until we had gone somewhere I could use the facilities to fulfill my compulsion. As we left the store she grabbed me into her arms overwhelmed with joy and just thanked me for the considerable concern I had just demonstrated for her. She was still yet in store for another surprise that was to come because it was Friday and we know that the eagle flies on Friday and its time to get your party on. As we began to drive I was headed for Molly's place and instead she asked me would I take her by her father's house. I asked where does he live. She told me and I headed in that direction, when we got there she introduced me to him and her two brothers, her father was a real down to earth person, he had a lot of game in his sack. He was a bonified player driving a spanking brand new Cadillac and his house was hooked up very nice with a bar and recreation room in the basement. As I talked with him we began to get very tight as we talked I learned that he was playing with three women up under his wing at the same time and they were paying his bills and making the note on his Cadillac every month. As we continued to talk her older brother was behind the bar listening to myself and his father's conversation, so he could consider how much game I had as a young man. He asked me what I wanted to drink. Their bar was full of all types of brand named liquors. I said I'll have some whiskey, so he fixed me a drink and then another and another. The runt had been upstairs taking a shower washing away all the tricks impurities that she had taken on that night before. After she freshened herself she put on the new outfit that I had purchased for her earlier. When she made her entrance down stairs her father looked her over as though he had not seen her look this glamorous before, then he complimented as to how nice she looked while he was adjusting her collar as not to show any breast, then he asked me where were we headed that night. I told him I was surprising her with a night out at the Masonic Temple a place where you danced and heard different singing groups perform. We started to leave when her father said have a good time and be careful out there. I said you don't have anything to worry about because I know just about everyone there who has a little game about themselves. We arrived at the Masonic Temple at nine thirty and I parked around the corner from it in a dark spot, as we entered the building and got searched by security guards we then went over and checked our coats. It was very crowded that night so I took her by the arm and began to mingle. I introduced her as my queen to everyone I knew, and she was feeling real proud to be with me and happy about all the attention I was showing her. We began to dance and all eyes were on us as we graced across the floor. We danced on every record that night keeping her close to me so no other dude would approach her. Then it was time for this high light show featuring the Dramatics, they had just come out on the scene and they had a forty five record out called What you see is what you get. They did a dynamic performance singing their hit single and making their debut. Little did I know at the time that they were going to become one of the most prominent groups known for their fantastic sound world wide? After their show was over we were preparing ourselves to go, so we got our coats and left. And we went and got in the car, we sat there and talked for quite a while then she told me that never before had she met a person with so much tender love and care like me before, and that she'd never forget the good times she had with me that day and night. She said you're just so full of surprises that I never know what you're going to do next. Then I reached in my pocket and said close your eyes, and she said what are you up to now? I said just close your eyes and you'll see, so when she had closed her eyes I took her hand and slipped a phony crackerjack box diamond ring on her finger, she opened her eyes and looked at the ring in absolute joy and she reached over and kissed me. Then we began to feel each other's bodies anxiously and then I pulled at her clothing trying to get my hand in her vagina, she said wait, and then she pulled down her lower garment and removed her panties. I pushed her down and pulled out my penis and immediately laid on her trying to guide my penis in to her hairy vagina. She reached her hand down and took my penis and directed it inside her where she wanted it to be, and we were dramatically pursuing our highest ecstasy that we could reach, my balls were rapidly banging against her buttocks, and her vagina was snapping rapidly on my penis. I was sixteen a young man full of energy and vigor and she was twenty-one, and I knew how to work her vagina with the utmost experience, so I persevered and continued to pump my penis in the right areas to amaze her. I knew whole heartedly that this act of intimacy was in affect going to have to be one of the best performance I could possibly engage myself in, it would determine her submission and respect for me by annihilating her vagina until she rendered herself helplessly venerable in my arms, we carried on with the sex until the windows on the car were all fogged up and no one could see inside nor could we see out, finally she gave out a big moan of satisfaction she had reached a superb orgasm, and I knew my job was complete but oddly enough who ever thought in there wildest imagination that I of all people would miraculously lose my virginity to a hoe. All in all every thing was going on without a hitch with me going to school and working at my co-op job every two weeks. And this would continue to remain a unknown mystery to all that thought they knew me well, and every thing they thought there was to know about my lively hood. It had come to the point now that the runt was starting to become very persistent continually insisting that she wanted me to spend more time with her, and she said that it seemed like the only time she would get a chance to see me was when I would come to grab up the money from her, which she had busted her behind trying to make for me, I told her not to think that I was taking her for granted, and that I'm not grateful for what she's done for me, but there are many other things that are priorities in my life that I am pursuing with haste, and that being said you have to acknowledge and take in to consideration that my whole world doesn't revolve around you. Now if you want to remain the queen of my stable, baby you had better adjust your attitude and continue to keep on racking in the doe to keep your man happy, cause baby the reality of it is if you can't produce the dollars and be satisfied, then all you're doing is taking up space for some other young worthy hoe to come in and prove herself a star. She had no idea that I was still pursuing my education in school, and as long as I have a say so it would remain that way.

Evelyn

Then I met this real sweet honey at school named Evelyn and I was trying to shoot my lines up on her and grab her up for the taking. I had went to visit her at her home where she stayed with her father and a Pilipino step mother as her mother had died in her earlier age, so I was sitting and talking to her and asked her did she want to go for a ride around bell isle seeing that I was driving my fathers old fifty-nine dodge. We continued to converse about the possibility of driving out there. So she went into the kitchen where her father was and asked him if it were all right for her to go out and hang with me for a while, he angrily said you're not going anywhere with that slick head nigga, she instantly rebelled at his attitude and immediately called him a black mother fucker, and he began to chase her, as she ran past me I remained sitting on the couch, he stood on the porch calling her to return back to the house, but she wasn't about to come back while he was in his angry state of mind,. I heard her calling my name as she stood down the street, so I got up off the couch and walked out on the porch where her father was standing, at the time when I went out I wasn't sure if he was going to try to intimidate me into an altercation with him, but instead he had his attention focused on his daughter Evelyn who was still standing down the street calling me, and beckoning for me to get the car and come and pick her up. So I walked down the stairs and got into my car and began to back it up down the street where she was, and she then entered into the car and we began to drive, neither of us really knowing what we were going to do at that moment. Suddenly out of no where as I was coming to a stop sign her father came up behind me driving erratically on my rear end. She saw him approach us and screamed panicking, drive she said don't let him catch us please, drive faster she said, I said calm down I'm stopping to see what he's got to say, trust me I won't let anything happen to you, he stopped and got out of his car and angrily walked up to my car door on the side where Evelyn was sitting, she screamed again and said I've got to lock the door, how do you lock this door she said? I reached over calmly and locked it for her as he stood at the car door. She was very frightened and shaking as he knocked on the window, at first she was reluctant to let the window down, then I said let the window down and talk to him, so she let it down slightly and he began to talk to her telling her to get out of the car and come home, she said no I'm to afraid, he said what do you think you're going to do, now listen to me get out of that damn car he said and she said no I'm not getting out because I'm afraid of what you might do, then he said in rage with anger well you just go ahead and let that lil punk nigga take care of your ass, he then walked away and got in his car and drove off. He didn't know me and didn't attempt to try and get a chance to know me. But little did he know that he willingly had just thrown his darling lil daughter into the diligent hands of a young bonifide pimp. I decided we would head for my domain while I tried to figure out what I was going to do with her, as we were driving she began to confide in me by telling me that her mother was a Pilipino and had died while she was a young girl. And that her father had been a career military solider, and was now retired and when her mother died he went back to the Philippines and got himself another Pilipino which was her step mother, and she continued by saying her and her step mother don't get along with one another and that she can't really stand her. As we got closer to the eastside where I resided in Detroit she asked me could we go by a girl friend of hers that lived over in that area, I said ok and we went over to pay her friend a visit, when we got there from my observation her friend was nothing but a sluttish hoe, but I couldn't object to her because all in all that was her friend and I speculated by that old saying birds of a feather flock together. I was beginning to have second thoughts about making her my main lil cutie because of her association with that lil slut, I started to think maybe she's been in the streets and had already gave up her virginity , but I really couldn't be sure of it, by judging her by who she liked to hang out with. When I told her it was time to make a move, I asked her did she want to stay all night with her friend, she replied no, I want to be with you and go where ever you take me, I still had no idea what I was going to do with her, but I knew one thing and that was that I would have to make sure that I keep a tremendous distance between her and the runt, after weighting my options for the situation that was at hand, there was only one solution I could derive for the problem, and that was for me to find a safe place where I could put her and myself up for the night, so that we could rest assured and deal with one day at a time regardless of what the outcome of tomorrow might bring, at least for that night and that night alone we would be together sharing what ever lil happiness we could find in one another, regardless of all the mishaps and turmoil that had improached upon us that day, so I came up with one alternative, I would let my brother in-law register us up in a motel room up on Mack avenue. I drove the car back to the house to keep my father from getting in an uproar with me. When he saw me pull up with Evelyn in the car he became suspicious. And he then started to question me about her. So I began to explain the circumstances evolving around her and the outrageous attitude her father had directed towards me, and how she had no one she could turn to in her moment of need, and that I would have to make some kind of arrangements to insure that she would have a place to stay that night and that in all probability I would have to stay with her and remain the whole night through, to ensure her that she wouldn't be abandoned by me, and comfort her, feeling that this whole troubling incident wouldn't have occurred if it had not been for my insisting that she ride out to belle isle. But now it had happened and there was no turning back the hands of time, I had to fess up and take on this responsibility like a man, my father was a lil angry at my decision but at the same time he also could understand my decision, but he wasn't pleased at what this mess had come to, so without any consolation he just said I hope for your sake you know what you're getting your self into, then he said you just make sure you don't take my car away from here , it was something I was already expecting him to say anyway. I told Evelyn to come on and we started walking towards Mack. When we had reached the corner my brother n law was there to greet us, with a big grin on his face as though he was saying in his mind, I know lil brother is going to have a sexual good time tonight. At the time sex wasn't really on my mind, my real concern was to provide a place for her to rest and figure out what tomorrow was going to bring, my brother in law gave me the key to the motel room, I then asked him to buy me a bottle of wine silver satin with Kool-Aid, that was the thing at the time, after he had gotten the wine and grape

Kool-Aid I told him to make sure that he doesn't tell the runt where I am or anything about this girl, because I knew he had a big mouth worse than a hoe so I had to put a double check on him. We went into the motel and the clerk was sitting at the desk and for some reason he didn't even raise his head up to pay any attention to us, as we opened the inside door and went up the stair case to our room. As we entered the room both of us began looking around to observe the room seeing that this was the first time she ever had been inside a motel room before. Afterwards we sat on the bed and she began to play and wrestle with me, I was glad she had been relieved of some of the terrible things that had taken place that day. She began to take off her clothes every thing but her slip, and then laid down and got under the cover. She looked so vulnerable and innocent laying there. Then I said you haven't had any thing to eat today have you? She said no I haven't eaten anything all day. I then picked up my kool-aid and poured it into my bottle of silver Satan and put the top back on and shook it up real good, then I took me two good swigs from the bottle as I was indulging with my drinking I asked her what would you like to eat some shrimp or a chicken dinner, seeing that we were just right next door to dot and Ettas a shrimp and chicken restaurant frequented by every one with a little game in the area. So I took another swig of the wine to build up my ego and make me feel like I could take on any body. So I said to her I'm getting up out of here, did you say you wanted the chicken dinner, she said yes that's what I'd like to have, I said I'll lock the door behind me and be right back, as I exited the motel entrance there were a lot of pimps and players occupying the space in front of the motel, as I started to walk over to the restaurant, I heard them making encouraging remarks to me, such as you got the best hand little brother, or do what you got to do and pimp on little man, and take care of your business, I just gave them a high five sign by raising my arm with my fist balled up in the air, I continued to walk after I had reached the restaurant I made my order and after it was ready I paid the lady and walked back to the motel. As I past the same pimps and players I played myself hard to the core as I bumped and pressed my way through them which earned me respect in their eyes, and I could see them looking me over in my sharp clothes that I was wearing. Yes there was no doubt that they respected me because some of them knew me by my relationship with the runt my star hoe, and I had no worry of them telling the runt that they had seen me enter a motel with another little honey, because that was the pimps code which was never to snitch on another pimp or player unless they were going too try to penetrate the stable. And another thing I was most noted for was my walk; I had a very sexy but dominating walk that earned my respect from every one. As I was about to enter the motel I briefly said later to the pimps and players standing outside, as I stepped inside I spoke to the clerk as he raised his head and replied back then I went through the other door that lead to my room where my little honey was awaiting my return. I turned the key to our door and announced myself so she wouldn't be frightened when I came into the room with our chicken dinners. I asked her was she afraid of being alone while I was gone? She said just a little, but I knew that you would soon be back. I laid the dinners on the bed and said help yourself, as I went over to the table where my wine bottle was at I picked it up and took me a nice long swig of it and sat the bottle down, as I watched her little mouth chewing on the food I could tell that she was hungry, she said you had better come on over and eat something with me, it's really good, I said I'll be over there in a minute, I then picked up the bottle and gave myself a long swig until it was empty then I put it down with a satisfaction of a nice but mellow high. Then I walked over to the bed and began taking my clothes off as she watched my every move, looking at me with a lustful intent and desire, I then laid on the bed and began eating, and she said why don't you get up under the cover so that I can get close to you, and she reach over and put her arms around me, I quickly finished eating a piece of chicken that I had in my hand and got a napkin out of the box and wiped the grease off of my hands. And then I reach over and pulled her body against mine and we began kissing erratically and then I climbed on top of her and continued kissing her, as my hands started pulling her slip up that she was still wearing, and I discovered that she had already removed her panties, so I took my penis in my hand and stuck it straight into her vagina and we began to have a very dramatic intercourse, she was extremely into it as she rapped her legs around me and I continually pumped her in an up and down motion, that's when I began to realize that she'd never been with a man before or had sex. So we continued to drastically romance one another for about an hour, and then I removed my penis from inside her vagina and rolled over and said we had better get some sleep because it's going to be a long day tomorrow, as I dosed off, it couldn't have been no longer than half an hour, when I felt her little hand touching me and calling my name, I said what's going on? And she replied don't you want to do it again? I said yea I do and immediately got on top of her and this time she took her little hand and grabbed my penis and she directed it where she wanted it to be in her vagina, she was slowly catching on how to have a intimate sexual encounter, I had an intercourse with her for about another hour, when I finally stopped and got off of her, and said now lets try and get some sleep. I turned over and once again began to dose off, once again a little hand was touching me and she was calling my name, and again I asked her what was the matter, can't you sleep? She replied to me by saying don't you want to do it some more, I said um-huh, and once again I climbed on top of her and placed my penis into her vagina and this time I said I'm going to lay it on you like you've never had sex before. We were engaged in a vigorous, steaming sexual expression with an intensified seduction. I engaged my penis deeper and deeper with every slight motion that I would perform on her. Suddenly I felt my penis slip deeper into another area of her vagina, and she moaned and groaned uncontrollably, as she locked her legs around me holding on to me with all her might. I could feel some hot slimy semen surrounding my penis as I continued to protrude into her vagina, she had been aroused to the point where she finally felt an ecstasy and had circum to a delightful orgasm, as I raised up off from her I looked down at her vagina and saw that the sheet was full of blood, she was laying there with a smile on her face telling me how much she loved me. When I saw the blood I knew I had been her first love because she was undoubtedly a true virgin. And now I had been the one to take her virginity away from her. But it was a satisfying feeling at that moment I felt real proud of myself of what I had accomplished. We finally got some sleep and woke up the next morning laying in each others arms, I told her it was check out time for us to vacate the motel, so I said lets get dressed and make our way out of here. So she washed herself up and got dressed, I only washed around my penis area, I told her if I was you I wouldn't wash my face with theses old contaminated motel towels cause there was no telling how many hoes had washed there vaginas and stinking asses with them, so with my compulsion act I couldn't bring myself to wash my face with the towels, but she did the opposite and washed her face and her entire body. I said it's up to you go on and do what you want to I have nothing else to say about it. We left the motel with neither of us having any idea what our next move would be, then I asked her what's on your mind? Exactly what do you want to do now? She said I'm going home and I hope my father has cooled off by now and hopefully is very worried about me. We started to walk down to the house and take my fathers car, but he had already very sternly told me as long as I was with Evelyn I had better not move his car, so I said we've got to catch the bus down town to get you in your right destination toward your home. So we caught the Mack bus to downtown and we were not able to sit with each other being that the bus was over crowed with people, but she was sitting in front of me on the opposite side and she continually turned her little head around to look at me with a loving smile on her face. We finally made it downtown and I waited with her to catch the bus that would take her home to an uncertain situation, but she was willing to face the problem head on whatever the outcome was going to be. Her bus finally arrived and she sheded a few tears as I released her from my embrace and she said I'll call you when I get home and let you know what happened when I got there ok, I said alright I'll be looking for you to call me, and then I kissed her and wiped the tears from her eyes, and said I love you baby girl and don't you forget that. I caught the Mack bus and went back towards my house, when I got off the bus and began to walk home I ran into an acquaintance of mine that knew the runt, and she told me that the runt was upset and had been looking for me all night, and had even been to my home in search for me, now she had made a big error because we had an understanding that under no circumstance was she ever to come to my parents home looking for me, that was a big no no. I was enraged at the thought that she had been there and disturbed my parents who was already upset with me because I had gone and stayed out all night with Evelyn. After I had gotten home my mother told me some old girl came by here looking for you about two o clock in the morning, ramping and raving like she was out of her mind. I told my mother that I already knew about her and I assured her that it wouldn't happen again. then I went upstairs to refresh myself, I took a nice long bath, and poured alcohol in my bath water, I just kept washing and washing myself, I just couldn't stop I had a compulsion of cleanliness and continued to rub my body until I had almost washed the skin off of me, finally after about an hour in the tub I came to a since of contentment and satisfaction. So I got out of the tub and dried myself off. And then I briefly went through my wardrobe and selected an outfit that was to my likeing, and began too get dressed. All the time I was thinking about Evelyn and what she might be going through with her father. But there was nothing I could do about it the situation was absolutely out of my hands, all I could do was to wait on her call, so I thought what would be a alternative to do while I wait for her call . So I decided to take my father's car and ride by and see Rochelle seeing that I had not been in contact with her for nearly seven months. So I drove by to see her when I arrived there I was not prepared for what I was about to see, as she came to the door and her stomach was so big it seemed as though it was about to burst, she politely asked me to come in so I stepped inside. Her mother was in the kitchen preparing supper. I spoke to her and she replied back to me with a smile on her face. Rochelle asked me if I wanted to have a seat, so we sat down on the couch and began to talk so that I could get some kind of idea how this came about and she told me that she had tried to put me out of her mind thinking that I didn't want to have anything to do with her any longer seeing as to how long I had vanished out of her life and wouldn't return any phone calls to her, so she met this guy and they became well acquainted. I knew the guy she was talking about and I never really cared about him in the past and now after this I really had a bad attitude toward him. She asked me if we could take a ride so she could get out and breathe some fresh air? I said yes so we drove for awhile, then I decided to go by my sister's place and relax for awhile, so we made it by there and my sister seeing me with a lady knew I wanted to be alone for sometime so she got her stuff together and told me that she'd be back later and if I leave before then just make sure I lock up everything. My sister was very dear to me and my best friend, whenever I'd have a woman that I was trying to get up on I could always rely on her to allow me to use her place to get my action on. After she left we sat and talked, the more I talked and looked at her it started to become intriguing to me. The thought of how it felt to have sex with a pregnant woman something I had never done before. So I started to run my hands up her legs and began feeling her vagina and the more I kept it up the more her panties became moist. So finally I pushed her back on the couch and began to undress her, and then I pulled out my hard penis and began to slip it into her vagina. She was so wet down there and very hot till I could not control myself. I just began banging my penis in and out until I finally came and I found a satisfactory relief. I found that it really wasn't any different than having sex with a woman that wasn't pregnant. I then took her back home, and assured her that no matter what the circumstance or outcome would be I told her that I would always have a place in my heart for her. So she got out and I left going by the house to check and see if Evelyn had called yet, when I got there I asked my mother did I have any calls? She said nobody but that girl that's been trying to catch up with you. I knew that was the runt. Then I decided that I still had a little time so I might as well run by Shirley's house seeing that I hadn't seen her in about five months since New Years Eve. So I went by her home and knocked on the door her mother came and answered it and said hello, I said hello back to her and then asked her was

Shirley home? She was just grinning at me with a big smile on her face as she asked me to come in and have a seat, then she went up the stairs calling Shirley's name as she made it to the top Shirley met her on the landing and began to slowly come down the stairs when she finally reached the bottom I couldn't believe my eyes. I said to myself not again, first Rochelle and now her, seeing both of them pregnant in one day was beyond belief, as she sat down, my lips were silent. I didn't have the fantast idea what I could say to her. My mind started wondering about the intimacy we had New Years Eve, but I also remembered that I did not penetrate her vagina, and I thought about the older guy who had been watching us as we entered back into the house that night and how I had felt that he had gotten her high off of something because that night she wasn't really acting like herself. I had no words to say to her and I knew she realized whose baby it was and that it was certainly not mine so without hesitation I just got up and politely left out the door. Afterwards as I drove off I felt sorry for her, and was feeling bad about the way I had just got up and removed myself from her presence, and I thought how glad her mother was to see me as though she thought I had arrived to take claim of the unborn child. I went back to my home to check and see if there had been any attempt of my little honey Evelyn to try and reach me. When I got there before I had a chance to ask, my mother quickly told me that Evelyn had called and told me to get back in touch with her as soon as I received her message. So I immediately called her home and she answered the phone and when she realized it was me she anxiously told me that she couldn't talk about what she had to tell me over the phone, but she needed me to come over as soon as I possibly can. I told her as soon as I contact my sister I would hurry and come over. So I hung up and dialed my sister's number and she answered and I began to explain to her about the circumstance evolving around the tempered attitude her father had toward me and how she stayed all night long at the motel last night and had went back home that next day with no idea to what was in store for her when she returned. My sister said do you plan to go over there? I said yes I do. She said well I'm going to tell you like this, you don't need to be going over to that lunatic's house by yourself, just hold up until I can get in touch with my husband and we can ride over there with you in case anything goes down between you and her father. I want us to be with you so we can help you take that sucker down, because I just don't feel comfortable with the idea of you being by yourself. So I went home to wait and see if Evelyn called me back, and to wait on my sister to get over there with her husband, and while I was waiting out of nowhere the runt popped up over my house banging on the door. I opened it in anger and stepped out on the porch to talk to her because what I had to say to her was not meant for my mother's ears. So I said to her what in the hell is your problem, everywhere I go I've been approached by someone telling me that you've been franticly looking for me and that my best bet was to get in touch with you immediately, if I don't want you to be going through some type of drastic changes and then I looked at her and reminisced a quote from Pimp the Story of my Life by Iceberg Slim. When one of them made a toast at the Players Ball, I said listen here runt. After she had accused me of throwing down with another young honey to take charge of her place and become my queen hoe. I said before I touch a square bitches slit, I'd suck a thousand clampy pricks, and swim through liquid shit, they all have puck between there rotten toes, and snot runs from there funky nose, and I wished they'd all become a sifislic wreck, and fall through their own asshole and break there mother fucking necks, she looked at me with her mouth hanging open trying to analyze and comprehend what I had just ran down on her, she had no Idea how to respond to what I had just said to her. Then I looked at her and told her with all that being said bitch you better be showing me some kind of respect and make those green backs for me, and get up out of my face with all your bullshit, before I put my foot deep in your ass. So she reached in her bra and pulled out a wad of cash and handed it to me and then she began saying I'm sorry I acted like a fool, and I hope you'll forgive me baby, cause there's not any thing I wouldn't do for you. I would rather die then to lose your love because you mean the world to me. Then as I calmly counted out the money she had given me it only came to a little over a hundred dollars I gave her a stern look and told her if your ass hadn't been running around chasing after me and trying to find out if I was laying with some other chick, you would have done better then this little bullshit and said you're slacking up, what's the matter is your tired ass getting to old to rake in the dollars? Maybe it is time to bring in some young tender honey to show you exactly how easy it is to make that fast money and in doing that I'll be very happy she said baby don't do that please give me another chance to make those big bucks for you, I said alright now get your ass out here and get busy and prove yourself a star. She left and went back over to Molly's to get busy. I stayed at the house waiting for my sister to touch base with me, finally she showed up at the house with her husband and we loaded up in the car and started on our way over to Evelyn's, when we got there we didn't know exactly how her father was going to act. Then Evelyn informed us how things were laying with her and her father, she explained to me that she was going to be moving upstairs with an elderly woman, seeing that they lived in a two family home, and she said that the lady upstairs knew her circumstances between her and her father and the problems she was constantly having with her step mother, so she made a proposition with her and she was going to let her rent a room from her for five dollars a week, and she said that she was getting out of the house that night and she would need us to help her move her bedroom set and clothing upstairs, when we went toward her bedroom to begin the task of moving her, her father was sitting in the doorway as if he was daring us to touch any of her merchandise as if he was going to try and raise up on me, but my old crazy brother in-law let him know immediately that his presence there was in no way any threat to us, my brother in law just went right up to him and pushed the chair he was sitting in right out of our way. Her father realizing that he wasn't dealing with any chumps and seeing that he would get beat down without any hesitation and toss him in an ally, he quickly changed his attitude and perspective toward us he hastily moved his chair out of our way like he had some sense, because it was either he get out of harms way or we were going to step right down on him, we moved all her items upstairs that night and helped her to get it situated. After we had finished she asked me if she could ride with us and hang out with me, I told her you just moved in with this nice lady so I think its best you stay in this night and put on a good example for your land lady and don't have her thinking that you're going to be running in and out all hours of the night, also that you're not going to have company coming and going like crazy, so after I had explained the complete issue with her she said you're right I'll do what you said and then she walked us down to the front porch where she gave me a big hug and kiss then she said you're coming over tomorrow aren't you? I said yes I'll be over tomorrow as soon as I get off of my coop job and make it home to bath and throw me on some of my fancy clothing. The next day my sister and my brothers girlfriend was throwing a gambling party over one of my associates crib, so that day I got off my coop job and changed clothes I went over to see Evelyn, and when I got there we went up to her room which she was renting up stairs, we sat out on the balcony with her on my lap, I stuck my hand down in her panties and played with her vagina, she became very aroused, and said lets go get in the bed and make love, we went in and laid down, then I began to undress her and I also got undressed myself, then we began to have sex. As soon as I put my penis into her vagina she immediately had an orgasm, I continued to thrust my penis into her rapidly, and she came again, she said baby don't stop, and really the truth is I wasn't about to, I continued thrusting my penis into her until I had screwed her dry. She rolled over and said baby you really know how to satisfy a woman, and I told her that the sex was better this time then the first time we got together, I knew it was because I had opened up her vagina, when I took away her virginity, so then we washed up and got dressed. Then she asked me could we go by her girl friends house and pick her up, that was the little slut she had for a friend? And I said it's alright with me. So we went over and snatched her up and began to drive away. I decided that we'd go pick up my home boy Glynn so he could spend some time with her girl friend. So afterwards we road around just hanging out and drinking, and Glynn was really starting to get up under my skin, he was trying to influence Evelyn to drink some of the wine which I was against knowing the affect that it might have on her, so he was really getting on my nerves. After I had told him not to give her anything else to drink, he just kept right on pouring it down her throat and Evelyn was beginning to seem like one stupid heifer, by her not ever having anything to drink before in her life so I assumed. Then Glynn started beating on her friend and telling her you're going to be my woman, he never really had any game about himself when it came to women; the only ones that would be attracted by him were some old sluts and ignorant women. But the more he beat on her, the more Evelyn laughed, she thought what he was doing was cute. That's when I realized and picked up on her attitude I saw that she was one of those women that wanted her man to be in control and whip her ass from time to time, and keep her in check. I found that was the only way she felt that she was getting attention, and that was by putting a good ass whipping on her. Between Glynn whipping on her friends ass and telling her, you're going to be my woman, and by him pouring wine down Evelyn's throat as she giggled and laughed, as she watched the confrontation going on between the two of them, I knew that it was just a matter of time before she got wasted off of the wine and some weed they were indulging them selves with. But I stood by the rule that I'd never smoke any weed after I had a bad reaction with it once in the past. We stopped up at Dot and Ettas to buy some shrimp or chicken, I figured if Evelyn got something greasy down on her stomach that it would help her sober up. But she was already to far gone because no sooner had she eaten a couple of shrimp, she ran out of dot and ettas straight to the alley, I went out behind her with concern for her, and as soon as I turned into the alley behind her, she had to let it go and threw up everything it seemed she had eaten that day. And slowly sobering up I said shut up that whining and whimpering because you brought all this mess down on your self. Just remember how I kept telling you over and over to stop drinking on that wine bottle, but you wanted to be hard headed and continually let Glynn persuade you to keep right on drinking. Then I said I ought to kick your ass for not listening to me, then without hesitation I slapped her up side her head and knocked her down, she was crying down on the ground and holding tightly to my pants legs, and then she said I'm sorry baby I won't disobey you again, then still angered at her for letting Glynn influence her over me, I struck her again up side her head while she was crying and still on the ground, and I told her now that's the language that you understand and that's a real live ass whipping, she said stuttering from her drunkenness I'm sorry baby, I'll listen to you from now on and I'll do anything to make this up to you, I said get your sorry ass up from off the ground, and lets go back to my house and clean you up. After she had washed her face and splashed some cold water on it she was beginning to feel better and not feeling that horrible drunkenness, when she came out of the bathroom she was just about back to being her same old self, and she came and set next to me and started rubbing on my hand, and I said that's right baby, rub those hands and remember what they're capable of doing to you. Then I said seeing how you like hanging out with hoes so much, I just might as well turn your little ass out, and then I left that alone for the time being. It had gotten late so I figured that it was just about time to bounce over to my sisters gambling party, before we left I had went down in my basement and reached up into the ceiling and pulled down a shoe box which inside was a pound of weed wrapped up in plastic. I had come by the weed through my brother just prior to him going to prison. He and his friend Lindsey had purchased it to sell on the streets and make some fast money, at that time you could get a pound of weed for less than two hundred and fifty dollars. So I got some aluminum foil and made up a pack of weed and gave it to Evelyn, so she could hold it for me, as we were on our way to the party, I let them roll up a joint to smoke, and I told Evelyn this is your thing smoking weed because you and alcohol don't get along, as we got to the house and started walking up toward the door, they were buzzed up till they were laughing and giggling tremendously, then we entered into the house. I was shocked and stunned, I had not in my wildest dreams imagined that the runt would be there as big as day. She was sitting at the table playing cards. I just casually took my companions and sat them down in the front room, as to make sure that I kept a distance between the runt and my new found honey. Not really knowing how the runt was going to react to this scene. So I walked into the room where the runt was, I talked to her as if there was nothing going on out of the norm. then I took the runt in the bath room and rolled up three joints, and then I asked her what did she have for me, she reached in her bra and pulled out a small wade of money and handed it to me, then she said baby can I have a little money to gamble with, I had not yet counted it up so I had no ideal how much it was nor did I really care, without hesitation I peeled off some cash and handed it to her, then I kissed her and we walked out the bathroom and went back to the table where she was sitting with my sister, so I handed each of them one of the three joints I had rolled. As I did this the dude that owned the house went off on me, saying you mother fucker don't be bringing no weed in my house and selling it, while we're in here trying to make money from a gambling party. At the time he didn't realize that the young lady I was speaking to was my sister. I had knew of his reputation of how bad he was and how once when he went to his ex-wife home and demanded that she turn his son over to him, and when she refused and wouldn't open the door for him to come in and get his son, in anger and rage he struck the door with his fist and it went completely through. She called the police in fear that he might knock the door down, so this was passed on by word of mouth as to how much strength he had and that he was capable of knocking a mans head off with one fatal blow, so as he continued to curse at me and going on about the weed incident, I said if you feel that way about it man I'll just raise up out of here, and then to my surprise the runt spoke up on my behalf. And then my sister and my brother's girlfriend got into the act and they told him that I don't have to leave, we're the ones that's throwing the gambling party and my sister said you better slow your tone down while you're talking to my brother, and then he said like what are you hoe's going to do to stop me from beating his ass, and the runt said you just try it motherfucker and I'll slice you up into so many pieces that they'll have to get a shovel to pick up your body parts. Then he attempted like he was about to get up in my face by that time Glynn who had been pretty high off the weed, when we first arrived was coming down and beginning to take on what was happening, he eased up behind him and picked up a heavy object that was in the house and the runt had came by my side and said now let me see you back up all you tuff talk. Next thing you know Glynn had busted him in the head with the object that he had picked up and I struck him in the face with all my might and the runt began slicing him up. I struck him once more to drop him on the floor and this time that fool finally hit the floor and as he laid there my sister and my brother's girlfriend started stumping him with their high heel shoes and he was just laying there moaning and groaning and all the people seeing what was going on at the party they were attending fearing for their own safety began to raise up out of there, so I told my sister and the others to leave with me to make sure that once he got himself together he wouldn't try to retaliate against them so the party had come to an end, and we all left together, as we loaded up in the car I didn't have any idea how the runt would react to the presence of Evelyn, so as we began to drive off laughing about how we had just kicked that punks ass, then I asked them where did they want me to drop them off, and the runt said you can drop me off at Molly's and she asked my sister and brother's girlfriend what were they going to do, my sister said I guess we'll be hanging with you, so as we pulled up in front of Molly's the runt said that motherfucker didn't have any business getting up in your face and disrespecting you like that, and I want to let everybody in the car to know that don't nobody disrespect my man or try to play him any kind of way. Right then I knew she was directing that remark to Evelyn, and then she leaned over the seat and gave me the money I had given her to gamble with. As Evelyn looked on then she gave me a kiss and they got out and went into Molly's and I pulled off. First I shot and dropped my friend Glynn off. I had just about enough out of him being still angry at him for influencing Evelyn to start engulfing herself nearly to death after drinking all that potent wine, I took Evelyn's hot ass slut friend home after I had contemplated whether I was going to add her to my stable or not, and I came to the conclusion that she was not worth the trouble because she was to strung out on weed and a drinking habit. Then after making those runs I started on my way to drop off Evelyn. When we got to her place neither one of us was saying anything all the way there. Finally she said who was that lady? I said that she was my queen hoe, and then she said are you going to turn me out and put me to work? I said baby first let me say when I laid my eyes on you all I knew was that you were one of the most beautiful women I had ever seen and deep down in my heart I had a feeling that I just had to have you and I wanted to just build my whole world around you, but as fate would have it after tonight I saw a new part of you which came out. I saw how you were easily influenced and how you were tremendously getting off on watching Glynn brutally beat and terrorize your friend with his immature behavior as to how a real man should treat their lady. And then the fiscal drama that I had to go through with all your bull shit reaction of your susceptible manner you incurred by the devastation of an ass whipping. I'm going to tell you like this baby I don't have anytime to be dealing with a woman with a perverted mind and likes to have her fantasies fulfilled by brutality, and the worst part of it all is that you have a bad habit by being strung out on weed. Now baby right now at this moment I just don't exactly know what I'm going to do with you, so I've got to think on that for awhile, number one and the most important of all you've got to kick your weed habit and I'm only giving you two weeks cold turkey, and if you can't kick your craving for your weed then that will let me know that the weed has a stronger hold on you than I do, and that you wont be any use to me by being my main love in my life or either walking the streets turning tricks twenty four seven. After that I visited her several times at the room she had rented up stairs from her father. Then I became suspicious of her behavior she thought she was fooling me but by her carelessness she had mistakenly left her little roaches in her ashtrays. I didn't confront her at the time, I still had some feeling for her, and then one day the runt called and said she needed to see me and it was very important that we meet. I told her I would be around there later that night when I got there it was something about the way she greeted me that brought on some suspicion that this was not going to be a friendly romantic excursion. As I was about to sit down and talk to her she brought that to an abrupt halt and she said lets go to the car where we can talk freely, so we went out to the car and I said lets ride to the liquor store so I can get a bottle of wine as we drove to the store she began to speak saying you're still seeing that young tramp aren't you? I said what does that have to do with you? She is someone who provides me with a different feeling something that you cant supply me with and anyway I don't see how you let that bother you as long as I'm continuing to satisfy you with your needs. Then she said didn't I tell you when we got together that I would be yours and do what ever it takes to make you happy, but I also told you one thing that I would not accept and that was for you to find another woman to take my place or rather should I say a tiny bopper, a youngster who could never do the things for you that I can, and now you're going to have to decide whether you want to stay with her or be with me and you best be careful how you answer because I always keep my word and I told you once that I'd rather be dead than not to have you in my life. We began to drive back from buying the wine at the store where they let people not old enough to purchase it. Then she said what's your answer going to be, and I said, first thing is you can get it out your mind if you think I'm going to let her go and if you can't accept that decision that I've made you can just bounce and I wont have anything else to do with you ever again, and then in anger she said don't think that you're going to get off that easy, cause I told you that I'd be prepared to die if I couldn't have you, but I'm also going to take your ass with me and without any warning she put her foot on top of my feet pushing down on the accelerator as hard as she possibly could while I tried to refrain her and fight her off. It was looking like she was going to keep her word and take us out, as the speedometer went up to fifty miles an hour, then it went to sixty, with me desperately trying to keep control of the car with us side swiping several parked vehicles. Then the speedometer reached a deadly seventy miles an hour. I was continually striking her in her face but it was to no avail. Her words had come back to hunt me and her desire to take our lives was proving itself to be true, but all I could think about was trying to cheat death and not go out like a punk. I was determine to survive as the speedometer reached eighty miles an hour with the car swerving recklessly down the street from left to right. I was drastically trying to maintain the car with all my driving skills to prevent us from having a devastating crash, but my attempt was effortless. She was determined to take us out together and it seemed she was undoubtedly about to succeed. As we neared a four way crossing with traffic being quite heavily active, I knew once we made contact with the crossing that if we made contact with one or more of the vehicles passing that we were not only going to probably end our lives, but some others also. My only chance of bringing an end to this madness she was demonstrating in anger towards me and not kill innocent people was to turn the car very sharply and as I did the car went into a drastic spend until it was finally brought to a stop by an old oak tree. With the runt being thrown through the front window and crashing her little body, breaking every bone as I sat in the car watching her helplessly. I only sustained glass cuts with nothing being broken; God had blessed me and spared me, for what purpose I did not yet understand. All I knew was that an accident of that magnitude, no one was suppose to survive, only if it had not been for that mighty intervention of Gods unchanging hand. When the ambulance and police arrived they announced the runt dead on the spot from the strong impact, and then the police interviewed me and I explained to them what had happened leading up to her subsequent death. They tried to give me a hard time and make me say that I was speeding on my own, but I continued to remain telling the same story over and over again until they finally decided to accept my version because truly that was the only version that they were going to get seeing that they had no way of questioning the runt by her being deceased and the title owner of the car, so they took her frail lifeless body downtown to the City Morgue and as I watched them bag her body up I was deeply affected trying to prevent this night from occurring and the runt losing her life, but I was grateful and kept on thanking God for his mercy he had shown me that night, after I had attended her funeral and paid my final respect for my queen a precious jewel, who was my little runt, my life changed. I vowed to God that I would walk in the path of righteousness. So the next day I caught the bus over to Evelyn's place and was not shocked to see her sitting out on the balcony smoking weed and entertaining a couple of guys. When I entered her room I looked at her very sternly and told her to lose those guys or I'll do it for her. She told them that they had to leave because there was something she had to do. I said to her why you didn't just be truthful with them and tell them that your man told them that they had to get up out of here. She said I didn't want to get anything started if I could prevent it I said it wasn't anything going to get started except for them getting their ass beat. After observing her walking around in their presents half naked I knew she had to be having sex with them and no telling how many others she had fucked in the past, I just came to the conclusion that my once adorable lovely little cutie was a weed head and sex fanatic with lesbian tendencies. I picked up one of the roaches of weed they had left laying in the ashtray. She had just demonstrated to me that she showed no respect to her landlord. The woman who had come to her rescue when her behind was about to be thrown in the street, and she just took none of that into regard. As I looked at the roach in my hand she said what's the matter baby? I said you don't know, I mean are you that naive to the point till that weed is burning your brains out and distorting your mind, truth being told you are the problem and it's a real sad shame that you can't realize it. Do you remember our conversation I had with you and how I had expressed my concern over you and your tremendous habit you had for your weed and I told you if your addiction was to come. before us then I would cut you lose like a hot potato because then I would know that your love was greater for your weed habit than it was for me, and that I wasn't going to try to compete against it, and let you have your weed and get up out of my way and my life, so baby girl that's all to say straight up without stuttering, that whatever we had between one another is gone and blowing in the wind and can never be recaptured or have me to look at you the same, so baby plain and clear we're through and you just lost the best thing that ever could have happened to you, and when I walk out that door you're going to feel the greatest emptiness and regret that you could have ever felt in your life, so good by baby . So I left and as I walked away I looked back and saw her standing out on the balcony in tears, softly calling my name and asking me to return. She never realized that I'd really abandon her.

Cleansing

After dissolving myself of all relationships I turned once again to my first love God. I gave myself to him day in and day out. I was now seventeen and I had sold all that weed I had in my basement ceiling. It was something that I was very reluctant to partake in my life with but I had to eliminate it from within my reach so there would be no perils to distract me from my commitment for God. I had made enough off of my weed venture that I had earned me enough to purchase me a brand new Cadillac, something that all the other guys I knew could only dream of but for some reason I was not anxious about the idea of buying one, at that time the selling price for a brand new fully loaded Cadillac was only in the range of approximately twenty five to three thousand dollars but seeing that I still had an half of semester of school left before I graduated from high school, and with the money that I was making and saving from my Coop job, and the money that I had made off the runt along with the money from the weed sells, I had a very large bank account where I would let it remain. As a young child I had envisioned money and all kinds of fancy jewelry falling in my home as the ceiling opened up and the window of heaven had openly relinquished to me, also I envisioned myself having a sixty seven Mercedes Benz, it was a vehicle so beautifully designed with all of the large chrome bumpers and its thick coats of shining paint. Those were just a few things that I had desired to own one day. It was strange that on my birthday while walking down the street when I had reached seventeen, something distracted my attention from what I was concentrating on in my mind, when in my view was a brand new sixty-seven Mercedes Benz and I just marveled at it as it took my breath away with its supreme beauty. At the time I could not afford to own one because the price range ran any where from nine thousand to twelve thousand dollars to purchase but inside I knew that one day I would have my beautiful luxurious dream car and my mind began to wonder and I thought about how the bible taught us that Gods time was not our time and what ever your heart desires if God had it in store for you can no man cast asunder, and I knew how Gods ways were not our way, and I knew I must trust and be patient and wait on the Lord.

Ida

I was riding the bus home from school one day when I was captured by the sight of a very beautiful but shy young lady. I approached her after making contact with her. I asked her could I sit next to her, she replied it was alright with her. I then sat down and introduced myself to her. I asked her was she coming from school seeing that she had a lap full of Books. She said yes. I said yea what school do you attend, thinking that she was a high school student? She said I attend Wayne State University. I said oh you do, that's real nice, how long have you been going there I asked, she said this is my third year. I said no kidding you really don't look that old, she said I guess I can take that as a complement. I said that's for real cause I never would have had any idea that you were attending college and especially for that period of time if you hadn't told me yourself. My stop was coming up shortly so I just came out and asked her for her phone number not knowing if she was going to realize my age, but she really didn't know if I were coming from school or work because the way I would dress for school sometimes I would be in one of my working uniforms and this particular day I met her I was wearing one of my work uniforms. So when I asked her she wrote her number down and handed it to me. I took it and got up preparing to get off the bus at the next stop and I bent over and whispered in her ear, I said you believe in love at first sight, well now I think I do because I felt cupids arrows hit me and it really did hurt so I guess the rough part of our relationship is over and it can only be smooth sailing uphill all the way from here, and you can be looking forward to that call from me, I can promise you that cause baby you're something special, and believe me it's true because in the blink of an eye you stole my heart and I don't want you to ever go so until then I'll be thinking about you, bye and I got off the bus and watched her as it pulled away. Later that day my friend Raymond who was on the bus at the time I had met her Ida was her name, he informed me that since he had to ride the bus a little farther than I did he had tried to see if he could get a chance with her and tried to get her number and snatch her from me. But he said man I don't know what kind of lines that you laid on her, but she wasn't giving up nothing to me not a number and not any action, he said man you got that girl rapped up tight. My obsession for God continually tore at my very heart I could not let God go because he was embedded in my very being, no matter how much destruction came my way trying to destroy the love I felt for him he would be there to lift me up, when I'm torn down he's brought me out of dark clouds, my God had invested him self in me and was not going to let me go, until I had what ever it was he had in store for me, Ida was special, she was not like all the other girls that I had associated myself with. She was as pure as snow when it first falls on the ground and is not tainted by any filth. But unfortunately she had met me at a bad time in my life where it was not promised that I would live to see another day. In the past I had taken down some of the badest dudes on Mack and beat them down, and had gained a reputation up on Mack.

Ricky

One night I had a unnecessary confrontation while me and a group of hard core dudes that followed me were hanging out, they were not just your every day bad guys, they were bad to the core and had no respect for life. I had met one of them through my sister when back in the day I was hanging out with the runt at Molly's, this guy named Ricardo had just been released from prison after serving over ten years for murder. He knew my sister through her husband while he was serving eighteen months, he had showed Ricardo a picture of my sister and he fell in love with her at first sight. So when he got out he was desperate to see her not caring what her husband had to say about it, because he considered her husband a punk when he was up in the joint. So when he met me over Molly's he immediately became tight with me, and became attached and very close, then he turned me on to his home boys who were also all hard core criminals and had served hard time in prison. First there was his right hand man who was in the joint with him, he was a very tall muscular man, and then there was little brother who was dangerous as they come, and last there was cousin who was very deadly and would take a life with out blinking twice, and they were all much older than I was but they took there orders from me. And this particular night when this confrontation occurred we were up at top hats, a hamburger joint really this altercation was something that could have been avoided, but this particular guy named Ricky who I had the incident with, went for bad and walked in the shadow of his big brother who had put fear in the heart of all that walked Mack going as far back as when he made the news for beating up a nun at the Catholic school that he attended up to the point of him beating and stabbing a man to death out in front of the pool room, and when someone that knew him went and told his family that he was about to kill a guy, his father went up there to try an stop him, and he turned and stabbed his own father in the leg. From that day forth he and his father hadn't spoken. And he was also one of the first young dudes to start shooting up dope. So me and his brother were in a simple confrontation over me walking up to him with my hand out to shake his and give him a play, and he started off about me stepping on his shoes and pushed me back from him, I said what's your problem man I just was giving you a play and, reach my hand out once again, he pushed me away from him, and so I said well alright forget it man, he said forget nothing, you better just get your punk ass out of my face, I said what's up with you? What is the deal man? And he said lets just get it on and started taking off his over coat, I said now let's take it out side man, and we went out the door as I was taking my coat off. I knew that this fight I was about to encounter was going to define to my boys exactly what I had in me and would either loose respect for me, or rather earn more highly respect from them on a much larger scale. As we left out the door I handed my coat to one of my mellows that was with me the next thing I remember is that we both manned up, and he came in swinging at me like a mad man, but I held my own , and was able to land some hard blows back in retaliation, after recognizing my fighting ability he stayed his distance realizing the power in my punches, but suddenly he once again lounged at me, this time he was trying to take me down to the ground. But he had no ideal that he was like a fly caught in a spider web seeing that wrestling was one of my better accomplishments, and by me getting him in a head lock was my best hold of defense. As I grabbed him around the head I tossed him down like a little rage doll, slamming his body to the hard concrete I then began to stump him and beat him with multiple counts of blows to the head, he then struggled to turn over and tried to get up from the beating, he became subjected to my blows to the back of his head, but he continued to have the strength of a mad man, and that only made me pound him even much harder. And my man Perkins the big fellow found it humorous as he took his knees and placed them with his head between them, and little brother started punching him in the head, as Perkins held on to him, I had enough of this brutal beating which I had punished him with, so I was about to get up off of him when suddenly I found some one putting a knife in my hand, and I heard a voice that said finish him, and I had just about raised my arm up about to come down with a fatal blow from the knife, when God stopped me and my conscience began to bother me, so I tossed the knife back, and said it's over man, and got up and told Perkin to let him go, and as he was getting up he was rambling on about how I was a dead man, and that I had better not walk down Mack again, I said just go head on while you can man, and as he continued babbling on Perkins kicked a big dent to his car door, and as he tried to escape from more abuse, he collided his car into one of the steel poles in the hamburger parking lot, and then sped off angrily, enraged and beaten down in disgrace. My mellows had seen me in action and there was no question in their minds as to my ability to handle myself, and this in its self had gained me much more respect from them than ever, and none of them would ever go against my authority, this at the time gave me a sense of pride without any thought or concern of the vicious threats which had just been made against my well being or on my life at that matter, they asked me if I wanted them to walk me to my house, I replied and told them that it was ok, because I had another run to make not realizing or caring about the danger that laid in wait for me out there in the darkness of night some where. After starting on my way back home from where I had visited, my uncle Fell pulled up and asked me where was I walking to that late at night and I said I was headed home, then he said I'll take you there, as we drove I explained to him what had taken place earlier, and he immediately responded and said with that mess you've just been involved in you defiantly don't have any business out here this late at night walking that long distance from my house to yours especially by yourself with what you just told me it wouldn't matter if you were with any one else any way because this other fellow seems to me like a mad man or a lunatic that you're dealing with. As he dropped me off in front of my house he sat there to make sure that I had safely gotten in. the next day I went to school and got out and returned home without any incident, until later on I was in front of my house and I saw him speeding by me down the street, still not taking into consideration as to the threat he had made against me I decide I would walk up to Mack and meet up with my boys, but when I got there they were nowhere to be found, so I got with some other guys and chipped in on a bottle of wild Irish rose wine, we went around behind the building in the alley lot just as I had started to open the bottle and my attention was focused on that. Suddenly a guy named baby Gus yelled out busted with him not knowing the real circumstances, as a car cruised in the ally way blocking us up against a dead end when I finally raised my eyes up I was startled when I saw that it was Ricky and four of his henchmen with him, my life suddenly flashed by me, then I regrouped myself trying to figure out how in Gods name was I going to get out of that ally alive, and I said God help me, and as Ricky began to walk up toward me I could see the gun in his hand, and I knew then that I was a dead man, and as he got closer I said naw man I can't go out like this and he said like a angry lion getting ready to devour his prey in a deadly voice he said yea man its over, as he was about to raise his arm and take aim with the gun, I took the wine bottle which I had not yet had a chance to take a swig out of it and threw it and struck him in his head, then I had to decided which side of the car would I take to make my escape, I looked on one side and that side looked to narrow for me to run and fight my way through, then I looked at the other side and began to run with Ricky shooting bullets at me that were ricocheting off the wall, I still hadn't noticed that the guy standing in front of me blocking my way was bobby his closet friend who had been with him the night of the altercation. Bobby was someone who I had also grown up with and neither of us had ever been in a beef before or had any reason to want to see either of us come to any harm, but I chose his direction as my only refuge of escaping death. So I plowed right into him swinging with all my might until he was down on his knees, and he continued holding me, and I was plugging blows at his head for him to release me so I could make my escape, and all I could hear was Ricky yelling frantically, you better not let him go bobby, you better not let him go he repeated it again and again, as he started to approach that side of the car, I then gave bobby one more forceful blow on his head and he let me go and fell over to the ground as if he was unconscious. I then made my escape and ran to the house, in all the excitement I had pissed in my pants from the close devastation with death. I finally made it to my house and my mother asked what was the matter, I explained to her what had just happened and asked her to open up her and my fathers footlocker where they kept important documents among other things like my fathers gun, I said I need daddy's gun momma open up the footlocker, while she was doing that I took off my pissy clothes and took me a bath and then I put on some clean clothing, after that I got the gun and put it down in my pants and told my mother there won't be anymore running and I'm going back up on Mack and let it be known. So I started on my way and ran across my mellow man Glynn and then Ricardo Perkins little brother and cousin and we walked through the alley back up to the stroll Mack, right to this day I believe that Bobby let me go purposely as that he thought that Ricky and I should be friends and not enemies going at each others throats seeing that we had grown up all our lives knowing one another and now it had come to this point and time now that we were in a deadly pursuit from which one of us wouldn't survive. Me and my boys walked down Mack stopping in the barber shops leaving the word that there wouldn't be anymore running, and went in all the pool halls and left the word that there'd be no more running and also left word in all the liquor stores and the after hour joints and hoe houses that there'd be no more running. I left no place anywhere he could possibly know about or where he might frequent without knowing by me bringing my stern rebuttal to his threat, so that he wouldn't have any excuse to rectify my action I'd be taking out on him when and if he crossed my path, as time wore on and the darkness was beginning to fall we split up and went our separate ways. Ricardo and his fellows had already left a strong check on his older brother the night before when he walked into a dope joint they were in and they approached him and told him who I was and that there had better not be anything that goes down my way concerning me, and if they even get one little word back to them about anybody attempting to harm me in any kind of way whatever it may be, they will come back with a hard retaliation. So that night when I had gotten in with my friend Glynn, we were enjoying a bottle of wine together when I glanced out the front window and saw Ricky's car pull up outside my house with his brother sitting in the passenger seat as he began to exit his car his brother remained seated as he walked up toward my front door I quickly ran up the stairs and got my fathers gun from out of the Foot Locker where I had returned it when we got in, but not knowing what this visit was about or what kind of attitude he had his mind set on. I wasn't about to take any kind of chance. When he knocked I said who is it? He said it's Ricky. I said what do you want man? He said I want to know if I can talk to you. I opened the door and kept my eyes on his action and was watching his every move lest I make a mistake and let him steal me. He said can you step out so we can talk? I said naw man. If you want to talk to me if there's anything you have to say to me you can come in and say it cause everybody in here knows about the deal that went down between you and I. And plus, I wasn't taking any chances by gong out and while talking to him I should get ambushed by his brother. So he stepped in and we began to talk, and he said I here word on Mack that you've been out there looking for me. I said no, I wasn't out looking for you. I was out leaving a warning for you that it wouldn't be anymore running. He said well that's not how I took it I said well then you took it the wrong way, now I'm telling you in person that there'll be no more running and you can take that to the bank, cause I'm going to tell you man when you made all your threats at first I didn't take them to seriously until our confrontation in the alley behind the liquor store that day gave me a wide awakening. So I had to regroup and get my game together because first of all anit nobody going to tell me where I can and better not walk, and second if I know somebody is out there that's a threat to my life I'm going to get to them first and Glynn being high off the wine we had been drinking kept interrupting telling him look aint nobody going to put there hands on my man and Ricky kept asking me to do something with my boy. I would say cool it Glynn and we'd start talking again. He said I always thought you were younger then I was when you were hanging around my house with my sister I said and what's that got to do with anything that took place between you and I, and he said nothing really I guess, and then he said where do we go from here, I said I'm willing to go the limit as far as I have to go to bring this to an end. Then he said brother what do you say we put it to an end right now because I've grown to have a lot of respect for you, what do you say is it over? I said I'm game and we shook on it and I walked him out and watched him and his brother pull off and go on their way and after us nearly killing one another we in turn became best running

117

buddies. Now after all that was behind me and there was no longer any danger I felt free and safe to involve Ida in my life knowing now that if she was out with me that she wouldn't be in the line of gun fire. That day I finally decided to call her and set up a date with her to take her to the show Ricky came by and wanted me to hang out with him. I told him that I was taking a young lady to the show and that he could drop me off by her house. He said he'd do it so he asked me how was I going to get there and I told him we were going to catch the bus so he said I'll drop you off downtown at the show if I wanted him to. I said I didn't mind and I really appreciated it. So later that day Ricky and I picked up Ida and drove downtown to the show after watching the picture we left and walked around downtown and looked in some of the store windows when we had come to a jewelry store we browsed in the window and a diamond ring caught her eyes and she was very dazzled at it and looked at me and said when I get engaged I want me a pink diamond ring like that one. I just glanced at it because right now marriage was the last thing on my mind but she was special and different from any other girl I had been with and if I were going to settle down it would be with someone like her, we continued to walk to our bus stop and we caught the bus and got to our last stop and got off, and from there I walked her the rest of the way home and we kissed and I told her good night, then I thanked God for bringing someone so nice and caring as Ida was into my life and I promised that I would never have her going through any kinds of things, like all my previous ladies had been through. I told God that I'd never use her or turn her out she was much to precious to me for that. The next night Rickey wanted me to hang out with him and we rode out and hit a few spots, first we went by a drug house where his big brother who was feared by many was in the process of shooting up his dope, after we had spoke to him we left and went by a party that I had been informed about, when we got there I ran into a sexy lady that went to Wilbur Wright School with me who had been liking me for quite some time, after I had talked with her for a while, I told Ricky that she and I were going out to his Cadillac for some privacy, when I got her out there we entered the back seat of the car, she was very eager to get sexual with me, as we laid down on the back seat, I pulled up her skirt and then I pulled down her panties, she was very aroused as I put my penis into her vagina, we had sex until we were both sweating very heavily, after both of us had our climax, we discontinued and got dressed and went back in side, by this time Ricky was board and about ready to leave.

Lester

We left and started on our way to another destination, as we drove along, he said I'm going to take you by one of the most notorious bad dudes in the city, he said a day ago a guy had crossed him about some of his dope, and he punished the guy by throwing him out of his forth floor apartment window, and then he started shooting him from the window, as the guy struggle to try and get up off the ground, so Ricky told me to be careful and not to say anything to offend this guy or get him mad. As we got out of the car and went in the building and started climbing the stairs to the forth floor I was a little uneasy about meeting this guy, then Ricky knocked on the door and when the guy opened it, he immediately smiled at me and grabbed me into his arms and hugged me, then he said what's happening swee-pee that was a name which he had called me from back in the past,. It had turned out that I knew this guy very well, his name was Lester and he used to go with my sister, and they were almost in the process of getting married, I said what's happening Lester? He said every thing is good, how have you been and how is your sweet sister doing, Ricky seeing our close relationship we had, was very stunned as he looked on, he said you two know each other? I said man this was almost my brother-in-law. So we set and drank and they smoked some weed together, and then we finally left and went on our way Lester was later killed by the drug under world, they had put a contract out on him after claiming him to be a snitch for the Fed's and when they caught up with him, they were told to make an example out of him, so they broke every bone in his body one at a time so that he could suffer the pain, then they shot him in the head, and threw his mangled body up on top of some trash at the Detroit City trash yard. When I woke up the next day I had to go on my Co- op job and little did I know while catching the bus back home after work, that when I made my bus transfer that I'd run into of all people but Ida. As I was crossing the street I saw her standing there, I came over and greeted her with a hug being that she was to shy to kiss in front of all the people at the bus stop, she said are you just coming from work? I said yes, and of all things that could have happened I ran into you, this really was a good thing by me running into her on one of my work days, and to top it off I had just gotten my new work uniforms that I had ordered on my job with my name on them. Now there could never be any question in her mind as to how old I was, and she'd never learn that I was still attending High School, Fate had dealt the cards in my favor and all in all I had a full deck. I rode the bus with her until I had come to my stop then I kissed her and got up and told her that I'd be by later, so I got off the bus and watched her as the bus pulled away, I was still elated with the fact that she had seen me coming from work that way, now she wouldn't think that I was just a thug hanging in the streets and was never going to amount to anything, except serving time in prison or being strung out on drugs, we had been at the right place at the right time and now all those thoughts were dismissed and we could maintain a good relationship between us and now she would believe anything I tell her, there would never be any doubt in her mind about my life style and she'd never know about the past and how I had lived a life in the streets, she would only know what I tell her and want her to know, I cared for her and handle her like a precious jewel not letting any kind of problems that I may encounter come to her attention, because she was much to fragile to be troubled by any unnecessary things also what I liked was she went to church every Sunday and not once did she bring it to my attention or in anyway try to persuade me to join her at service, she knew it was something about me that was different and that God and I were united in our own way and I believe somewhere deep in her mind she knew that God had a special work for me to do but it was not yet time and whenever it be Gods will to use me I would be obedient and ready to serve him in anyway he chooses I will serve him without question, for God is my all, and it is in him I live, and in him I move, and have my being, and I was obsessed for God and could not let him go, for he had anointed me with the power of four and I strive on that power for my protection against evil, if it had not been for God I would not have made it this far, but by God's will I survived and was victorious over all the evil principalities of darkness by the power four I have survived.

Crossing paths again

It was a Saturday and some of my friends and I decided that we would go to Edge Water Park and hang out, so we went and got us something to drink before we got there and took another bottle into the park with us, we had been out there until the night had arrived, I was standing over by the Ferris wheel and drinking the last of the bottle, as I went to throw the bottle into the trash, a strange feeling over came me, as three white girls came by me laughing and giggling as they had just gotten off the Ferris wheel, suddenly without any control of my lips I spoke out her name and one of the girls stopped and looked at me and called out my name back, it was her, it was my little burned white girlfriend, but she was no longer scared from the fire, she was beautiful, she had a golden tan, and her hair was silky and long and her legs were long and shapely in her little bikini shorts she was wearing. I said I always thought about you and always knew that I'd see you again, we hugged and kissed each other and she said you haven't changed, you still look the way I remembered you, and we hugged again as though we didn't want to let each other go in fear that we might get separated in the large crowd of people moving continuously through the park, I said you look beautiful, she said thank you and started telling me about how when she reached the right age, how her mother allowed the doctors to perform the plastic surgery on her, she said it took almost two years and several operations and this is what came out of it, and I said a beautiful swan is what came out of it, I'm just amazed that out of all these people I recognized you and called out your name, I know it had to be a divine intervention by God, but I always knew in my heart that I would see you again someday and low and be hold here we are, our eyes began to search simultaneously for a place of refuge where we could be alone. We choose to occupy a deserted area behind the wall adjacent to where the Ferris wheel was set up. As we got there and began to embrace her hands began to roam until they had grasped at my penis and began to squeeze and tug at it until she had made me come to a complete arousement. She was desperately sticking her tongue down my throat, after thoroughly slobbering profusely inside my mouth, she finally decided to come up for air, and then she said isn't it wonderful how we crossed paths once again after so long of a time being separated, but she said I always had hoped that this day would accrue and I tell you it was absolutely worth the wait to see you and look at you now you're all grown up, as she was speaking she began to unloosen her bikini shorts she was wearing and pulled them down gently exposing her long golden legs and her hairy vagina, she then reach out at me and unzipped my pants and stuck her hand inside and pulled my stiff penis out, and gradually inserted it into her vagina which was already excessively wet from all the arousing excitement. Then her vagina began a rhythmic motion on my penis as her hands grabbed tightly on my ass and my hand responded by squeezing on hers, I became engulfed inside her hairy vagina which felt so stimulating which just farther aroused me even more until I could not contain myself from reaching down and grabbing her by her legs and lifting her ass up until she had her legs wrapped completely around my body. We were together at last without a care at all as to what was going on around us, as we continued to cling together with our bodies entwined in one another, she soon began to moan and I knew that I had brought her to a tantalizing unique orgasm, and at the same time I surcame to a delightful climax and released a ton of semen inside her vagina, and I'll remember that moment for as long as I live. I began to gently let her legs back down to the ground, as she bent over and put on her pants as they became drenched in her soaked vagina. And then she caressed and kissed me so tenderly then looked in my eyes and said for this joyful fulfillment I have just experienced, I could wait the same amount of years all over again just to achieve that moment once more, because baby you were amazing and everything I imagined you would be, we hugged and kissed again after wards we returned back to where her friends were waiting for her impatiently, so she called them over and introduced me to them, and told them that I was the guy she had talked about so much in the past, we said hello to one another, and they started insisting that she come on and go with them , she said let me give you my number and we started searching for something to write with and finally we got a pen from one of the guys working at one of the vendors and then she wrote her number and was handing it to me, with a big beautiful smile on her face as she said good bye to me, I watched her till I could no longer see her as she got lost in the crowd all I could do was to grin because I just really couldn't believe that I had just seen her and hugged her after all these years of wondering what had become of her. Then I stuck the number deep down inside my pocket, I did not want to lose track of her again after it had taken so long to find her and then I went walking around trying to catch up with my friends who I had come there with and after walking for a while I caught up with them but I decided not tell them about what had just taken place we continued to enjoy our selves at the park, until it came closing time, none of us realizing that the park would never be opened another summer after that year, it had been determined that the park would be dismantled and closed down for ever after that summer. It had been one of the first large amusement parks ever built in the country. When we got home I was high and tired, so I just pulled my clothes off and left them scattered all over my bed room floor. So as I slept that morning my mother came and gathered up my dirty clothes, and had began to wash before I had awaken, when I finally awoke the first thought on my mind was me running into my old little white girl friend, then I had to get my mind together as to rather I had been dreaming or did it really happen, and the reality of it was that yes! It had really transpired as I remembered. Then I could hear the sound of our washing machine running in the basement very loudly then immediately I looked with my eyes searching around my room and then I glanced at the floor for my clothes I had been wearing the day before, remembering that I had placed the phone number in my pocket, so in desperation I called down stairs to my mother, hoping and praying that she had retrieved the piece of paper from out of my pocket before she had began to wash, knowing that she usually always checked our pockets to make sure that we don't have anything in them of importance, as she replied back to me, asking me what did I want? I said mama please tell me that you checked my pockets before you began to wash, then she said I felt them and didn't feel anything in them, then I said you didn't happen to take out a little piece of paper from the pockets did you? She said no, I had no ideal that a little piece of paper was in them. She said you usually take everything out of your pockets when you get in at night, so I didn't check for a small piece of paper, I just felt them to make sure that I didn't feel anything and I couldn't feel a little piece of paper anyway, I said that's ok, she said was it something important, I said mama if you only knew how important it was you wouldn't believe it, but I said don't worry about it mama, what's meant to be is meant to be and I guess that just wasn't intended for me. I was still in disbelief, I had waited all these years and when it finally manifested itself something as simple as a clothes washing machine washed away all my dreams. I remained stunned for a while until I came to the reality, that without the little sheet of paper that there was no way of any kind that I would be able to get in contact with her, and a chance of meeting her again like that, is one in billion, maybe even one in a trillion, I had to let it go and get on with my life.

I believe it was for the best because it would not have been fare to Ida for me to begin another affair with some one else, seeing how I felt for her and that I wanted to be truthful to her in our relationship. Ida and I had an abstain affair we made love but we didn't have an intercourse. I was very particular when it came to her, I cared for her so much that I denied myself from having a sexual intercourse with her, first it was out of love for her, and respect, but most of all I didn't want to interfere with her obtaining her college degree, by her becoming pregnant and having a baby to destroy all the hard years of studying, by having to stop and raise a child. I think she was going to be the first child in her family to graduate from college and earn a Bachelors degree and especially graduating from a prestige's college as Wayne State. That was a very highly rated school that turned out nothing but the best, if you were able to continue to sustain and remain keeping up your grade average to enable you to be given government grants. And I was very proud of her more than she could ever imagine or know, because I didn't walk around with my chest stuck out bragging to everyone else, and throwing the fact that my lady was attending Wayne State and making like she's all this and all that because she attended Wayne State which in turn, had no interest pertaining to our relationship when we were together school was the farthest thing s on our minds, all we cared about was that we had one another and that's all that really mattered. I spent as much time with her that I possibly could, only with one inconvenience, that was me not having a car for transportation, but she was willing to walk when ever we had to go some where, but most of the time it was just walking from her house to mine and usually when she came over to visit, my father would occasionally let me take her back home in his new car. Finally after graduating from high school I got a job with Chrysler Corporation, now that I had a job I didn't have to keep her in the dark any longer. After a little less than a year at Chrysler I received my greetings from Uncle Sam and I served in the military during the Vietnam era shortly after serving some time I was injured and received an honorable discharge and was sent back home. When I returned home that night I immediately went around to my sisters house, where she had gathered together a small group of our friends and I drank and partied all night, it was good to be back home, and I was once again with my old running partner, my big sister. After getting a good rest that next day I bath and dressed and set out to walk over to Ida's house and see her we talked she was very glad and happy to see me once again I stayed over her place all the rest of the day and that night after we had made love in our own little manner, I got ready to leave and she told me you know you'll always have my heart, I went home that night and got some rest and when I awaken I didn't waste anytime getting back into the work force, I could have stayed out for ninety days before I returned back to work without being penalized, but I was on a mission and I didn't have a moment to waste cause by me having over ninety days on the job before I went into the service my job had under the government law to reinstate me with full seniority so I got reinstated and was right back on the job the day I returned , they were filming and taking pictures of the different type of jobs that went on inside my plant so my supervisor told me to stand at a job so that the paper could take a picture of me and have me in the newspaper of the plant for that month when it came out I remember laughing about something my father had said when he saw my picture in it he said I've been with Chrysler over twenty years and haven't missed a day and they have the nerve to put your picture in their paper, and your tail walked right in there and in one day after returning home from the service, they grab you up and take your picture and feather you in their monthly news paper, we all laughed at what my father had said, because he was really upset, but to all of us in the house it was one big joke. I was working hard and saving my money and I also had the money in the bank which I had gotten in the days I was hustling in the streets. Now it was just a matter of time before I would start looking at all the sharpest cars that came out that year of nineteen sixty nine. I had in my mind the choice between a Cadillac, Buick, or an Oldsmobile, those were three of the hottest cars on the market that year at first I thought about buying a used car and holding on to much of my money, but then I changed my mind when I was riding the bus and my eyes spotted a beautiful Electric two twenty five drop top Buick. When I saw it I just had to have it, there was no doubt in my mind that was the car. Now all I had to do was decide what color I wanted and my mind was on an Aztec Gold, my oldest brother and I went and picked it up, and I brought it home and parked it right in front of our house, every one on the block was looking and admiring it. I went in and got dressed and my older brother and the woman he was living with at the time was hanging with us, after I dressed my brother and I had our selves a few shots of liquor and we took the rest of the bottle with us, and headed for Ida's house with my brother behind the wheel driving. When we pulled up over Ida's house her entire family came out to admire the car, Ida grabbed her bags and we were on our way cruising around, we eventually ended up driving out to Belle Isle Park, and we found us a nice parking place by the river and we let the top down and had the music blasting loud as we set and talked and my brother and I indulged in a little liquor then my oldest brother said you know our brother is going to be released from prison in a month, he said you know he's going to worry you to death about driving your car. He couldn't be no ways farther from the truth, than as far as your eyes can see past your nose. Ida had grown worried about our relationship was going to be affected by me owning my new vehicle. It seemed her older sisters had shaken up her nerves by telling her, that you know by him being a young good looking man owning a car like he has, that every girl walking is going to try and get up next to him, and that I would be jealously envied by all the men and admired and attracted by woman of every kind, I told her she didn't have anything to concern herself with because I was always going to be the same old me, and I was not about to let a car change my way of living my life.

Brother

My brother was finally released from prison and his eyes were set right on my car, he could hardly wait for me to take him to the secretary of state to take his test to obtain his drivers license, when he first got them I was very reluctant to permitting him to drive my car, but by me having to go to work I decided to have him drop me off and keep it while I was at the job. I had hoped when he was released from prison after obtaining his high school diploma and a degree in philosophy and theology that he would be a changed man and straighten out his life and find himself a good job, and maybe even go to college and farther his education. But his eyes were on the street life and how to make that fast money selling drugs. When he was released from prison I gave him five hundred dollars cash money, which was an extreme amount of money at that time, it was to enable him to buy himself a new wardrobe, and this allowed him to have more clothes then guys that had already been out in the streets. Next thing I knew he was hitting me up for some money to rent a place, where he would set up a dope house, it was a prime location that he had chosen seeing that it was right down the street from Kettering High school, and most of the best customers were young students. We had a lot of the younger generation getting high at that time off of cocaine, that was what we sold as penny caps, he was making good money and driving my car around with people thinking it was his while I was at work at Chrysler. He would drop me off at work and I would ride back with my best friend Jerome who was married at the time, but he always loved to hang out with me which caused conflict between his wife and myself by her accusing me of wrecking, their marriage, but that was out of my hands because I couldn't control weather he wanted to go home after work or hang out with me. Sometimes we would go to this topless bar or either we would end up at the dope joint where neither one of us got high on drugs, we would just enjoy our selves a cold wine together and he also always had to have his Colt forty five beer.

Penny Cap Addiction

One day unexpectedly I dropped by the dope joint and was shocked to find my brother injecting drugs into his veins and getting high, that was a real let down for me because I was willing to go along with selling the dope, but I had no intention of my brother or my self getting caught up on it, but I guess I knew it was just a matter of time before my brother drifted in the world of being addicted to drugs. He tried to explain to me that he had it under control, but I knew better than that because back then the drugs were not cut, they were one hundred percent pure and any one who tried it once was going to be hooked from that point on. At that time mostly everyone was just snorting it up their nose, but eventually the next step would be for them to start shooting it up. We had two guys who worked and lived there with my brother, their names were Butch and John also along with them staying there were their women. Both of them were long time users of cocaine and they also shot it up along with their girl friends. I knew with the curiosity and the temptation of what it would feel like shooting up would soon catch hold to my brother and he would have to try it and see what the effect of shooting up was like and it soon struck his curiosity and he had become entangled with the world of getting high off of shooting drugs, and the worst thing about it is that you're using your own product and you would become your best customer, and all your profits you were making are going up your own veins.

But some how my brother was always able to have just enough money to get up on a new bag every time we ran down low. So it was just a dope house maintaining enough dope to get high and enough money to keep the dope coming through the door for the customers, we eventually had to put a cut on the drugs to make it stretch longer but that really wasn't good business against the competition of the other drug houses, unless we maintain a good relations with the top dealers, to give us their most potent package that they had available. My brother had met the girl who would become his wife during the first week that he had returned home, while we were attending a party given by a heavy drug dealer. She remained by his side through the entirety of his dope dealing days. My girlfriend Ida had spoken the truth when we were talking on the phone one night, after it had been sometime since she had seen me and she made a remark out of desperation as to how our relationship was slowly fading away, she remarked as my brother was calling me to hurry so we could go out in the streets and hang out, she said I'm so sorry to say this but your brother is taking you away from me, to this day those words still haunt me, and if I could turn back the hands of time, I would do it without hesitation, and would have let my brother live the life style that he wanted to live, and I would have taken my life in another direction and held fast to my beloved Ida. But as time would have it I indeed did drift away and I believe that was the last conversation that Ida and I would ever have until later in my life.

Rip Off

The drug house headed for a down spiral after one morning I had just left the joint and some acquaintance of my brother which he had known from the penitentiary came in and robbed it, John had opened the door and let them in at gun point, Butch was laying in the den unbeknownst to him that a robbery was occurring while he slept, then they went up stairs to my brothers bedroom where he laid sleeping with his girl friend, they took all the drugs on hand and what little money that was there and to top it off they took my brothers whole wardrobe, and then they said in a devilish way, where is your brother and his little gun? They knew when they had seen me in the past that I always carried around a twenty five automatic. Then they made off with their goods and made their escape out the back door as Butch awakened and realized to what had just taken place, he then quickly leaped to his feet and went after them in pursuit with his pistol fire ring at them as they ran to get in their get away car and sped away. When I got off work that night I found out what had taken place, and if it had not been for me just leaving before they had arrived, I believe in my heart that they would have killed everyone in the house, but by me not being present at the time and them knowing how tight my brother and I were, knowing if they had killed him and left me alive, they knew that I would not have rested until I had tracked everyone of them down that was involved, and killed them mercilessly.

Retribution

So that night we laid out our plans for retaliation, and how we would go about doing it. The next day we went to the pawn shop and bought two shot guns and brought them back to the house, then we cut the barrels off making them into sawed off shot guns, so that when we made our move on them we would be able to conceal them. Once we located them we went out in pursuit of them, we found out they were held up on the top floor of an apartment building, doing drugs and drinking just getting on with their high. What we had in store for them was going to be a total surprise, John and I stationed ourselves on the second level of the building, my brother and Butch stood their grounds outside the door, of where they were enjoying themselves with our stash, they had the music blasting loudly as my brother stood to the side of the door, Butch knocked on it, by us being the last thing on their mind that they would expect being there, as they carelessly began to open the door suddenly they realized that my brother was standing to the side, someone hollered it's them then immediately they tried to shut the door back, my brother jumped in front of it with his sawed off shot gun and fired, blowing the door half way down, but the sawed off shot gun had exploded in his hand. We knew that once they started returning fire back out of the apartment, that we had to come to my brother's aid, so we ran up the stairs with our guns and shot guns blazing, and I handed my brother another pistol and we continued blasting until there was nothing but smoke settling in the air, it was a terrible blood bath left inside, from the after math, our job was complete and revenge had been taken out swiftly and quick.

Stroganoff, womanizer and killer

And it wasn't long after that my brother started hanging out with a fellow named Larry, whom we had known all our lives but we never really hung out with him during our young age. Now he had made a name for himself, after spending some time in New York City. It had been said he had become a big dope dealer there and was nick named Stroganoff. That was due to his taste for the famous Stroganoff sandwiches, which he delighted him self with every day. He and my brother had made a name for themselves by ripping off the dope dealers and beating down anyone that apposed them. Stroganoff had a few women which he abused drastically if they didn't do exactly what he wanted them to do for him. On one occasion he had me to drive him over to my brother's mother-in-laws house, to check on his ex-wife who was over there visiting with them, almost immediately after entering the door he began beating her helplessly. My brother's mother-in-law screamed in desperation for me to intervene and come to her assistance. I grabbed Stroganoff off of her and struck him in the jaw. He immediately refrained from hitting her. After we had left she was sitting in the back seat of my car in fear of him, not knowing what he would do next. Suddenly he leaped over my front seat and began attacking her again. She screamed in desperation for me to assist her. I pulled over to the curb and opened the door then got out and reached in the back seat and pulled Stroganoff off of her. And then I began to beat him down. After wards he walked the rest of the way back to the house where my brother was waiting on our return. He got there before I did, and had told my brother a bunch of lies, about how I had attacked him while he was trying to check his lady. Stroganoff was known for his murderous trail he left behind him. But I was one person that he feared exceedingly. My brother and Stroganoff had come with a plan to rob the Syndicates main black numbers man in the city of Detroit. They put it in action and got excess into one of his business by an acquaintance that knew him and trusted him. Once they had excess they struck him up side the head with a gun and insisted that he open up his safe where they knew it had to be at least half a million dollars. Every time they would beat him to the point of him obliging them by opening the safe, some one would knock on the door to the business for the number man, then my brother and Stroganoff would have to let them in to avoid suspicion, what they would do each time they were interrupted they would make the women take off their panties and bras then use them to tie their hands up, once again they would begin beating Mr. White mercilessly trying to make him open the safe again, but he was very reluctant and with the confusion of people knocking on the door to gain entrance, and with them stopping all the time, having to tie people up with the panties and bras as they entered, they were soon frustrated and also out of panties and bras. They finally made their way to his office and found safely stacked away about two hundred thousand dollars in saving bonds, which Mr. White would buy from everyone around who wanted to cash in before their due date, there were also several thousand dollars in cash, with the place becoming packed with people tied up on the floor, and Mr. Whites resistance to corporate and open the safe, my brother and Stroganoff decided that they had better take what they had acquired and get out while they had the chance. Mr. White couldn't call the police and report that he had been robbed and there were not many dudes that would consider excepting a proposition from him to fill a contract against my brother and Stroganoff. Mr., White just had to bare his lost, because the syndicate was not involved with his side activity of buying the saving bonds. It didn't end there, Stroganoff had come up with a plan to set up one of his henchmen who had killed for him before, he had compromised with him to make an attempt on my brothers life, this was after Stroganoff found out that he had looked inside the brief case and seen the saving bonds and money that he and my brother had acquired from the robbery on Mr. White, and he wanted a part of it. Stroganoff gave him a gun with him not knowing that there weren't any bullets in it and told him to kill my brother once they had gotten in the car, and they would dump his dead body in an alley. With him thinking his gun was loaded, as soon as they got in the car with a guy named Spunk driving and Stroganoff sitting in the front with him, the henchmen and my brother were riding in the back, as they began to drive off, the henchman feeling assured of himself quickly pulled the gun from his pants and pointed it at my brothers temple and began to rapidly pull the trigger, only to become baffled when the gun did not fire, my brother quickly responded and pulled his revolver and immediately emptied the chambers into him, as he leaped toward the front seat and grabbed Spunk who was driving, he covered him in blood while he was desperately trying to escape from the line of fire as my brother emptied his gun into him, then to add to the drama Stroganoff pulled his gun out and also poured his bullets into him finishing him off. They searched for an empty alley and drove through it, but in stead of my brother's body being dumped the door was opened and they proceeded to drive along and push the henchmen's body out into the alley and sped away. Then they went to Boston where Stroganoff had some relatives were staying there, and they hung there until things had cooled down in Detroit. Upon Stroganoff and my brother's return from Boston, the police was already in pursuit of them by information given to them by one of the victims brother. It wasn't long before they apprehended them and charged them with murder. It was only a few days after that Stroganoff was out on bond due to the efforts of his lady friends and the assistance of his mother who idolized the ground he walked on. Still on our agenda was the necessity to make enough money to set the bond for my brother. Stroganoff and I got together and came up with a solution to make the fifty-thousand dollar cash bond. We decided to organize the government bonds they had stole from Mr. White, and seek out the recipients and take them to the bank and cash them and set them out a small fee for their corporations. This became a very tiring and weary feat, but only after a week of going out continually each day we had acquired the amount to make my brothers bond. They were eventually brought to trial after the police had found a little boy about ten years old to testify that he witnessed the vehicle they were driving as it sped in the ally almost running him over, as they dumped the henchman's body from the car, it only goes to show you what a person would be capable of doing for the little ten dollars witness fee.

It seems his mother was forcing him to testify so she could get that little money each day of the trail to help her with her to support her drug habit. As the trial proceeded the little boy was so fearful of my brother and Stroganoffs appearance and their demeanor that he could not look directly at them as the prosecutor pounded him with questions. After a few days of testimony the little boy could bear no more, and broke down crying on the witness stand and then testified that he could not be sure my brother and Stroganoff were the men he thought he had seen. The prosecutor tried relentlessly to get a conviction by cross examining the little boy one more time in a futile attempt to have him to point them out as the men he had previously said he saw, but the fear he sustained in a adult environment only brought him to tears once again, and at the direct questioning of the prosecutor he took back his testimony and under oft declared to the court room that he was mistaken and they were not the men he saw. My brother and Stroganoff were acquitted and released. After wards Stroganoff and my brother started a large drug distributing network. Stroganoff was getting over big time and was well known and feared throughout Detroit. He had purchased two luxury vehicles and quite a lot of property. He had runners selling his product, but one of them messed over his money and when Stroganoff confronted him he beat Stroganoffs ass. This did not set well with Stroganoff, he immediately sought to put a contract out on him as he had did to so many people in the past, but this time it was different and personal so Stroganoff decided to make the hit himself. At the time I was unaware as to what had transpired till one day I was approached by the guy's brother who the contract was out on. It turned out I had known this young man and his family all their lives, so his brother knowing the relationship that me and my brother had with Stroganoff, pleaded for me to intercede and save his brother's life, I informed him that I would look into the matter at hand, but before I had a chance to confront Stroganoff he had already put his actions in motion. A informant had told him where the guy he was looking for could be found, he immediately road down on him and began shooting at him right up on the main street of Mack Ave. the dude tried to crawl under a car to dodge the bullets, but Stroganoff was bent out on revenge, so he crouched down and started firing up under the car striking him several times in the body and once in the head. That night when my mellow man and I went to Stroganoffs place he was laid back sipping on a drink and listening to the record Alvin Stone the birth of a gangster by the fantastic four. Indeed Stroganoff was   undeniable a ungodly sick bastard. Stroganoff went right back into his womanizing ways, but this time he would make a big mistake, he got into a confrontation with one of his women, he was angered at his lady and began beating her relentlessly, and after he had beaten her he had the nerve to tell her to fix him some thing to eat. As she prepared his plate and brought it to him and he had started indulging in his meal, he never had any ideal that this would be his last, his lady had taken enough of his abuse and was not going to tolerate it anymore, so she went into the room and got a pistol and came back out nonchalantly and walked up behind him as he put the fork up to his mouth to consume another bite, she quietly pulled the trigger and blew the back of his head off, and with a smile on his face as he laid dead with his face in the plate. That was the end of the Stroganoff reining of terror, after all that he had been through in his life, he was taken out by a woman, and she didn't have to do one day for his death.

SISTER

My dear sister had now also gotten a taste of the dope world, and to support her hungering appetite she turned to bank robbery, once she had defied the odds of achieving a robbery on her own it became as comfortable and easy as slipping on a pair of shoes. The only assistance that she required was a get away driver and that would come to be me on several occasions, she would go in with her pistol in her purse with make up on and a wig on her head and pass the teller a robbery demand on a slip of paper sometimes if they seemed as though they were going to be reluctant she would have to become verbal and announce a hold up. Once she obtained the money in a bag she walked calmly out the door as though she had just made a legal withdrawal. Once outside she'd jump in the car and we would speed off before anyone would dare to come out and try to memorize the license plate number. After over twenty five daring robberies as fate would have it her time ran out and she was apprehended right inside the bank surrounded by a barrage of police officers. She went to trial and by it being her first offense she received three years in the federal penitentiary and my brother's time had run out on him. He caught another case and was sentenced to seven years in the state penitentiary. This was now his second time going to prison but far from being his last. I was alone but not without my God whom I had made a covenant with and he kept me in the closeness of his bosom and everyday I read my Bible, then when I finished reading it and was sitting in my quiet place a voice spoke out to me calling my name and I answered and then the voice sounding like a soft thunder said what are you doing? I said I am worshipping you Lord and the voice spoke again and said to serve me is to feed my children what you have learned of me. Now get up and go out into the world and share the word of God with all that come by you and tell them about how Jesus died for the remissions of their sins and gave them a chance for everlasting life, and I was obedient and straight way got up and walked out the door preaching the gospel to all men I came by and told them that I am one who cries out loud about the second coming of Christ take heed for heaven is at hand and I continued to speak about the goodness of God each and everyday. I arose and prayed without ceasing to the Almighty God. My sister was released from prison and I was glad she had heard about the work I was doing for the Lord and was pleased, but her time to receive the Holy Ghost had not yet come when she returned home.

Lennie aka Goldie

A guy named Lennie had just been released from prison after serving ten years for one of the worst notorious slayings in the early sixties. He had been a big time dope man called by the name of Goldie and he wore a gold tooth and had gold jewelry and drove a gold Cadillac, but he was a victim of his own product. He was selling and was taking large amounts of pills and cocaine. He eventually was losing his mind and would sit up in his house and shoot his gun and put bullet holes in the wall right over people's head that were sitting on the couch. He happened to accidentally shoot himself in the hand and some white boys that would come and buy dope from him saw his hand wrapped and asked him what had happened and when he told them that he had shot himself in the hand they began to laugh at him and said you must be a fool to shoot yourself and he got angered at them and said I'm going to let you see what it feels like and he began to shoot one of them after the other one had went out to the car he continued to shoot the white boy until he had run out of bullets. Then he loaded up the gun again and began to shoot him some more until he had emptied the gun again. Then he told his cousin to go outside and tell the other white guy that his brother in-law wanted him to come back in so he got out the car and went back in not concerning himself with the gunshots that he had been hearing because it was nothing unusual about Lennie shooting inside the house. But once he got in they took him to another room so he wouldn't see his brother in-law lying on the floor being shot over fifteen times. Then Lennie went in the room and began shooting him until the gun was empty and loaded it up again and emptied the gun on him again. When he was finished he had shot them both separately approximately twenty times a piece. Then he had every one that was there to help him carry their bodies out on his back porch balcony and that night Lennie took my sister and myself out on the back balcony to see the bodies laying there wiggling around with a little life still remaining alive and he kept them out there for a couple of days. Then he put them in their car and drove them away and pulled in an alley and poured gasoline on them and burnt them alive. Lennie was immediately arrested and charged for their murders and was sentenced and sent to prison where he continued to distribute drugs while he was serving time in Jackson prison. No one ever really expected Lennie to serve that short time of ten years he did considering the aptitude of his offense, but he was out and he had always had a liking for my sister back when she hung out with his sisters and now that she was divorced from her husband he didn't waste anytime trying to get with her. He would come over to the house every Sunday and would go to church and then come back by and sit and talk to my father all day trying to catch the attention of my sister affection. Eventually they started going together and he was coming by on every occasion he could. Then finally my parents were moving into a new house so they rented their other house to my sister, and Lennie didn't waste anytime setting up his drug operation there and he and my sister were becoming one of the biggest dope sellers on the eastside of Detroit. For some reason I cant begin to explain all the days and months and years that went by, my mind never once considered or thought about trying to make some kind of contact with Ida. During this time I was being disobedient to my God, I took up with over four hundred women, though this is something I am not proud of yet it happened, some of them were for a short time and some for a prolonged relationship, and everyone of them I did have sex with in the time that I was being promiscuous I caught the claps twice, and the crabs once, and had to pay a visit to the little red school house, that's what everyone with a little game called Herman Keeper hospital where you were treated for these type of disease

Various women in my life

The women I associated with were some of the finest women in the city and desired by all men. But I had a special attraction that would captivate them into my arms. There was Patricia, Darlene, Delyn, Cheryl, and then there was Shirley who I met through my sister, she was always proud to introduce me to her lady friends, she knew what type of women that would attract my interest, as she did in this case when she had told Shirley who was a friend of hers about me, and she asked her would she like to talk with her brother, so she gave me her phone number and I called her. Shirley was a white girl living in Dearborn in a very racist county just twenty five miles out side of Detroit; she was a friend of my sister who became very attracted to me after talking on the phone with me one day, so she wanted to meet me in person. That night I went to pick her up my friend Abdul rode out with me, and we were enjoying a drink of liquor as we drove on our way to pick her up, when we got off the freeway and entered Dearborn we were at a lost of what direction to go in to find her street, so as we rode along we pulled up next to a police car and rolled down the window and asked them for directions, they were very happy to assist us so we thought, we found the house very easily with their directions, after we got out of the car and went up on the porch, I knocked on the door her friend who was also white answered the door and let us in and told me that Shirley was still getting dressed and would be out shortly.

While we were waiting she offered us something to drink and her male friend that was also there offered us some weed I declined, but Abdul was glad to indulge himself. Finally Shirley came out of the bedroom, she was more then I had expected even though I knew my sister wouldn't turn me on to any one that wasn't looking the part, by her knowing what I liked in a woman. Shirley was tall and tanned a beauty to behold, she came over to me and I greeted her with a hug, we were compatible right from the start. As we left to head back to Detroit we went down a side street by her directions, to get to the Freeway quicker, and as we were about half way in the block about five police patrol cars blocked us in from every side, then the same police who we had asked for directions got out of their patrol car and approached my car, I rolled down the window and confronted them telling them that they know I haven't done anything wrong and that they know I wouldn't have been fool enough to ask them for directions if I were going to commit a crime out there. But I knew that was not the reason they had stopped us, but it was because we were two black men with a white woman in the car. He asked me for my I D and driver license, then some plain cloths cops came over to the car and told us to get out, we obliged them and got out, leaving Shirley still sitting in the car, they began too search the car and one of them came out with about twenty joints of weed in his hand, and said what's this? I said you're not a fool you know exactly what it is, but I'll tell you one thing you're not going to put that on me, cause man you know that you planted that in my car, then they said well which one of you dose it belong to, thinking it might have been Shirley's weed, I immediately told them take me to jail right now, and I bet you won't be able to prove that's mine, I said come on just take me to jail, they said I thought when you asked for directions, we had asked you did you have anything in the car, then they came out with about half a bottle of liquor and handed it to Abdul and told him to pour it out, Abdul said man is you crazy, you think I'm going to waste this good liquor and he opened it up and began to drink form the bottle, and then he reached over the top of the car and handed me the bottle and I began to drink from it, when suddenly one of the plain clothes cops that was there pulled out a sawed off shot gun and pointed it at my head and said, nigga if you don't put that bottle down I'll blow your head off, the cop that had initially stopped us feared for my safety, and said do what he says cause he hates blacks and he's killed them before, so I reached over the car and handed Abdul the little bit that was left in the bottle, Abdul turned it up and finished it, they then told him to get rid of that bottle, Abdul tossed it on some people's lawn, this infuriated them, they said don't throw that there, pick it up and put it in your car, they then began to approach me with their weapons pointed at me and one of them said nigga I'm going to kill you, he was raising his gun ready to take me out, when the other officer's grabbed him and held him back, then out of nowhere down at the corner a big black Lincoln pulled there and stopped and a white man in a suit was talking on a police radio, I guess they couldn't make out what type of guys we were, who had no fear of them let alone death, so I assumed the man down at the corner after listening in on our conversation over his police radio decided it would be best to let us go, so I told them to give me my license back and the other officer raised his gun in anger and shot off a round at me, he was so enraged, until the other officers had to restrain him, and we entered back into the car and drove off. When I tell that story to friends of mine who know about the racism in Dearborn they say man you give me a chill just talking about it, you know how close you came to losing your life, but I didn't let that stop me cause every night after I got off work I went out there to Dearborn and picked up Shirley and I never had another problem out of any of the policemen there. I believe the head man who appeared at the corner, that almost fatal night, gave orders for the officers to allow me to come and go as I pleased without any altercation. Shirley had no fear, she liked living on the edge. And it just so happened the first time we had sex was at this place in the middle of Dearborn called Hines Park where all the younger generation hanged out and did everything unmentionable. We stopped and parked I was feeling pretty good as I was sipping on a cold bottle of wine, then we got out and walked over by a tree and she pulled off her pants and I dropped mine and we had mad sex even knowing it was a very dangerous engagement, for all it would have took is for the police to see my black ass screwing this lily white girl up against a tree in an all white community, they would have blown me away without any question, and would have justified themselves by saying that they thought I was in the act of committing rape, and they would have walked free and after that I came out there every night to pick her up without any altercations with the police. I knew when I first laid eyes on Shirley I saw pimp me written right on top of her forehead. We had a very convenient arrangement. I would pick her up from Dearborn and bring her down to Detroit, and at night I would put her to work turning tricks up on Mack all night long, and then in the morning I would take her back to Dearborn so she could eat, shit and shower then get her ass some rest for another night on the strip. After her I became involved with another white girl name Nadia she was attracted to my looks and tall slender body and she also noticed my nice manner as I would come to the bank where she was employed, when I came to make my bank transactions. After observing me coming and going for awhile she made a desperate move to gain my attention, when one day I had made a transaction and had just left out the door, when suddenly she jumped up and took her lunch break and hurried out the door behind me calling my name, I stopped and waited for her to see what was on her mind then she began to tell me how much she admired the way I carried myself and she was very fascinated with me, that day she asked me would I join her on her lunch break, I said sure, I haven't got anything to do right now, so after she had eaten her lunch and I was taking her back to work she asked me would I pull over a few blocks away from where she worked, so I pulled over and parked, and she immediately without hesitation reached over and grabbed my head and began kissing as my hands started to move up under her dress and fondle her, she was a very beautiful young lady and had some very sexy legs. After we had caressed and kissed for some length of time, I realized it was time to be getting her back to her job, before leaving she asked would I come back and meet her when she had gotten off from work that day, and I told her that I would return. That evening I went back to the bank and met up with her, we left her car parked in a Kmart lot while we went to the motel and began to immediately have sex. I was banging her to the point of ecstasy and all she could cry out was don't stop, don't stop, oh baby please don't stop, which I really had no intentions of doing anyway, after abolishing her vagina she became mesmerized with my ability to please her beyond belief. We had an ongoing relationship for some time, with her working her nine to five job so that when pay day came around she knew exactly what I was expecting from her and she was always eager to provide me with some cash to keep in my pocket and have a little to spend on a motel for us to do the wild thing, and treat her to a meal out on certain occasions and plus it helped to pay my rent from time to time. This was right before I started to lose interest in her, partly because of her weed smoking habit and her insisting to see me more often, so I gradually stopped seeing her and would only go to the bank on her off days. Then something happened out of the ordinary, it seems by my father frequenting the same bank as I did, without any shame she boldly spoke to him one day when he was at the bank making a transaction, she was aware who he was by our last names, and she told him in front of all her coworkers, she said you had better tell your son to get in touch with me if he knows what's good for him. So one day while I was up at Kmart I ran into my father, and he looked at me very alarming and said do you know a white girl who works at the bank over there, by the bank being right across the street, at first I was startled trying to figure out in my mind how he knew about her then he said I don't know what she's up to but I think you better get in touch with her, because when she spoke to me the other day she sounded drastic. After giving it some consideration I decided my only option was to get in touch with her, so I called her and we made plans to meet. We drove to a motel and went in, took off our clothes and laid in the bed. I was lying on my back trying to figure out how I was going to break off from her. When she began to crawl downward and grab my penis and began to suck on it, after about a half a hour of licking on my balls and sucking on my penis, she stopped and crawled back up to where I was lying and I turned over and began to have sex with her. She began licking on my ear and then whispered in it. When is it going to be my turn? I said your turn for what; she said when are you going to go down on me? I said very quickly baby you've got the wrong guy. I don't know what other guys had done with you before I came along, but I'm going to let you know plain and simple that I don't go that way, and if that's what you're expecting then you've got the wrong person. Then she said I went down on you and you're not going to do me to? I said yes you did but I didn't ask you to go there, you did what you wanted to do, and baby if your feeling's are hurt I'm sorry, but you can wait till hell freezes over and I still wont go down on you. She got quiet as we continued to have sex, after ward we got dressed and left. I didn't try to contact her after we had that discussion but I think she got the point and I didn't have to be bothered with her any longer.

Murder by Association

I had affairs with over four hundred women in my life and as the years rolled by the majority of them died from a drug related incident, and all I can say, is what a waste, but there was one young lady that stands out in my mind who I became very involved with her name was Pamela. I had known her from Jr. High School she was not trying to be saved and give herself to the Lord.   Instead she was a dope addict and I also soon found out after she had me to run her over her friend's house and then drop them off on the strip I discovered she was a hoe and turned tricks to take care of her drug habit. I dropped her off one day and she asked me would I come back a certain time and pick her up so I said I would and after I had went back to retrieve her. It became a routine for me to make that run, but Pamela was in a breed of her own designated as her own pimp   for herself seeing that she first and foremost had to use most of her money to take care of her ever growing heroin addiction but she also had her a passionate side by showing her care and appreciation for the duties I performed for her by dropping her off and picking her up from the hoe track, and to show her gratitude for me making her feel safe she always tore me off a nice sizeable wade of money. Then one day she asked me to take her to a drug house so she could go in and cope her package of drugs, but the drug house was out of dope and she got disgusted trying to franticly think of another place she could go that had a drug supply with the potent quality that her body so badly craved for.   After going to a couple of other places she was still unable to get her package starting to have withdrawals she was in dire need for her body to absorb some dope so I finally told her about my sisters place. I was very reluctant at first to be a part of helping her to get the drugs her body so badly craved but I suggested that we go over to my sisters house and I assured her after she asked me was there stuff any good. I told her that they probably have some of the badest dope in town. So we went there and I greeted my sister with a hug. Lennie was upstairs getting high so I told my sister the situation and so she hooked her up a nice package and I told her you pay for it and get it yourself because I don't want to take any part of your transaction so she coped it and we left to go to her place where she could relax and shoot up but there was one problem she usually had the dope man to find a vein and shoot her up so she was getting desperately restless and finally asked me to be the one to shoot the dope into her but I declined and then she began to beg me to hit her up. She was almost bringing herself to tears. She continued to insist for me to shoot her up even after I told her I had never shot anyone up before, but she still insisted so I finally gave in and then she began to prepare her works. She tied her rubber around her arm to find a vein and then she began to cook her dope up and once she did that she took the needle and filled it with the drugs she had cooked up and all time she was complaining about the drugs better be about something and finally she handed me the needle and told me to shoot it in one of her veins. I searched her arm and found a very large vein protruding out and I took the needle and without hesitation stuck it directly into her vein and squeezed it into her arm. After it was empty I removed it and she took off the rubber strap and set on my lap saying that dope wasn't shit, that dope wasn't shit and as she was slowly drifting away she was still trying to mumble that dope wasn't shit then it hit her as she said that dope wasn't, and then she went off into a deep nod. I sat there holding her on my lap and then I began to get worried about her because her body became like dead weight on me so I started calling her name and shaking her. I finally got up and laid her on the couch, I went and got cold water and threw it on her but she still did not respond I didn't know what to do. I wanted to call my sister and ask her what should I do to revive her but I couldn't think straight at the time, I couldn't believe that this girl had messed around and O.D.ed. On me I couldn't do a thing for her I didn't even think about calling the ambulance or anyone. All I knew was that she had died by my hands being involved, and the only thing left for me to do was to drive away leaving her body behind with no association to me or any part I had played in her demise. I went home and was saddened by what I deemed as a very unnecessary misfortune brought on by the ongoing growth of a drug addicted society, which was consuming the lives of the rich and poor, black and white, young and old, it had no separation of gender its only objection was to enlist as many participants and introduce them to a ready and available substance. I went back into the depth of my Bible to seek out a reasonable answer to all the negative phenomenal of evil triumphs that had partaken in my life, and the dark had to come to the light to alleviate my perspective in a unsettled environment that surrounded me to escape the oppression and find the purist of pure environment to dwell and look to the hills from which cometh my help, and my help cometh from the Lord, so I reached out from within a desolate word to find my inspiration that God had allowed me to perceive that there would be peace and prosperity in a spiritual realm where there would be no division to separate me from Gods unchanging hand so I went boldly before the throne of grace, already knowing in my heart that my God was a forgiving God. He divided me from things of the world that I could perceive all the Godly things which he had in store for me. And I was taken back to the power of four and all I had inside of me was for the glory of God that being his mercy and grace and an everlasting covenant between he and I. Then I made another covenant with God that I ,might purge myself of the impurities of this world by depriving myself of meat or poultry of any sort that I may be perfectly cleansed that my God could enter into my heart without me having any mark or blemish to assure that this covenant would continually go on through out all the days of my life, and all my days I did give to God and did service unto him that he may smile upon me and be well please and walk with me all my days. I was enabled great power in the number of four by the grace of God. When you look at the Bible and relate it to numbers you will find that in Gods most omnipotent way the numbers play a great role in Gods plans, there is the number seven, twelve, twenty four and forty all these and more are many numerous spectacles in how God orchestrates. Let there be no doubt and a word of warning for any one who misuses God word for Gods way is not our way but what so ever manner that God uses to implement his judgment should not be taken lightly and should not be banished or discarded for God can talk through an ass then what other means do you acknowledge Gods greatness that can be performed.

Putting in Order

My brother was soon released from prison with his mind set on not ever having to return back to the penitentiary again, but things were not really going to well for him so he soon found himself caught up on the street game once again and he had caught another case and just when he thought things weren't going to get any better for him, he was blessed one day while walking down the street and he saw a job announcement placed in a store picture window and it was advertising for young men who might be interest in a apprenticeship for a pipe fitting job to fill out an application and they would contact you if you were accepted. Well by the grace of God just before he was to go before the judge at court on his pending case they contacted him and told him he was accepted. By receiving this good news it was brought to the attention of the judge and his case was dismissed and he began a promising apprenticeship career as a pipe fitter for four years on the job training and attending school in the evening he had finally found something beneficial and achieving in his life, but on the other hand things weren't going so good for my sister and her boyfriend Lennie. They had caught a case for drug trafficking and distributing and they had to go before the judge and Lennie was found guilty and sentenced to five years in the state penitentiary and my sister was released. I had met a very lovely young lady who I admired and enjoyed being in her company she came from our old neighborhood and by chance

I had picked her and her sister up one day and gave them a lift. I spent most of my time than usually with her, she was such a pretty petite little beauty and she was very attracted to me. By this time the auto industry was falling on hard times and they were cutting back and laying off a lot of workers and shutting down some factories completely, but I was one of the lucky ones. I had just enough seniority to keep me in the work force. So I continued to work until I was injured by a machine exploding on me and knocking me down from off the eight foot raft I was standing on, the machine shot a piece of metal through my helmet I was wearing, and struck me in the head knocking me unconscious, at least I thought I was because as I laid on the floor with my mouth kissing the filthy floor I heard laughter coming from over me and as I tried to raise my head up to see what was making this noise I saw it and I knew I was awake at the time. Standing there over me in his full array was Satan himself standing and laughing at me as I was helplessly lying on the floor. I really can't begin to describe him but he was colorful with bright colors of all sorts. It was a sight that no one has ever encountered, I believe accept for myself. He had come to claim me to do his beckoning lest I should die. I was weak and did all I could not to give in to the devils bidding he said to me just serve and worship me and I will give you life and all the abundance that your heart desires. I said no I will not worship you rather I should give up my life before doing so, and he laughed at me and said in your weakness you can not deny me what I ask you, then as I was about to fade away a voice said to me stroke your head four times with your hand, and I was obedient and immediately did as I was told, when I stroked my head it was so numb that when I touched it there seemed to be a missing part of me for I could not feel my head, but I did as I were instructed and the devil vanished. When I woke up I was at the hospital being treated for a concussion and then released and sent home. I was off of work for over three months. But I realized that on that day I had come face to face with Satan himself. I continued to read my Bible for strength in the Lord to defeat the devils aggression toward me and I was continuing to see my girlfriend until one day her sister accused me of making a pass at her. I talked to her and told her that it was not true but because of the accusation I decided to depart and stop seeing her. At about that time I and my friend Abdul were hanging out together and he was involved with the communist league and he was determined to induct me into the party, so I decided to attend some of there meetings. I eventually became involved, in it but at a meeting I had to question their belief so I said I cannot be a part of anything that does not believe that the Almighty God is the creator of all things and that he gave his only begotten son so that we could be saved and have everlasting life and it is through him that all things are possible not Marxist Lenin, Stalin and Chairman. Mao Si Tung and they adhered to what I had to say and told me we cannot change or take away what your belief is we only want to greet you as a brother so I continued to attend their meetings but I never made a commitment and joined the party but I met a lovely sister who was in the party and she was desired by all the brothers in the party but she had never given herself into any of them until I came along I was with Abdul over her and her girlfriend home where we had been having a meeting involving a wild cat strike. Some of the brother's in the league were protesting against Chrysler so we had been up for many sleepless nights.

Cassandra aka Smitty

So after the meeting was over Abdul seeing that I was tired said for me to relax and get some rest over their house while he and others go and take care of some business pertaining to our wild cat strike. So I sat on the couch and fell asleep the next thing I remember was a gentle hand taking mine and pulling me in the direction of her bedroom. When I got inside the bedroom we undressed, and we cuddled down together and automatically became sexually involved and from that day she became my lady and I was envied by all the other comrades. We were together a little over a year and a half and then one night I made a very stupid mistake I had been drinking and I came over to her mothers house to visit her where she was staying at the time, after her and her two roommates went on a renters strike against their landlord and was eventually evicted. So in the mean time she was living with her mother, so when I came in she was on the phone and the attitude she was talking in made me think she was talking to another guy so when she had finished talking and hung up the phone she slowly started to walk my way with her arms out to embrace me. I just barely stuck my arm out to refuse her embrace and she lost her balance and fell straight back on the floor. She was so enraged with anger she didn't give me a chance to try to explain, she immediately screamed for me to get out. I asked her to let me talk to her; she didn't want to hear a word. I had to say she screamed at me so loud her mother who was upstairs talking to her landlord heard her and came down and along with her daughter she asked me to leave, after pleading with them to let me explain what occurred and how it occurred. They just insisted that I leave so I went out to my car and it was winter time, but I slept in the car outside her home hoping to have a chance to talk with her when she leaves in the morning to go to work, but I over slept and she left without me having a chance to ask her for her forgiveness, so I drove off and went home and called her when she had gotten off work, but she just would not accept my apology. I continued to try to make up with her even trying to get her girlfriends to talk to her in my behalf, but she was not budging or giving in. I finally learned the magnitude behind her anger. I found out getting off work one night and some of the comrades were out at the plant passing out pamphlets and that's when one of them approached me and said you know you're going to be a father. When he said that I began to understand why she was so angry at me that night when the incident occurred. She was preparing to tell me that she was pregnant but I ignorantly ended that by letting myself become annoyed over nothing and now I was paying the price for it. I immediately drove over to her mother's house and knocked on the door all anxious and excited about becoming a father, but her mother came to the door and wouldn't let me in to talk to her, so I slept in the car outside her mother's home again. When morning had arrived I went back up to the door and began to knock, that's when the lady upstairs who was the landlord spoke to me and told me that she no longer stayed there with her mother, so I continued for sometime effortlessly to reach her until I finally gave up the fight.

Soul mate

I received a call from my little ex girlfriend when I had left after her sister tried to say I maid advances toward her. She was calling me to see if I wanted to go to a concert with her, I said yes, so we got together that night and once again engaged in a loving relationship while I had no idea what had become of the mother of my child I would never see nor hold but I found out it was a boy. I prayed to God to forgive me for being absent in my sons life, God knows it was not by my choice. Each day of my life I think of him and my heart feels for his well being, and I pray that all is going well in his life and that one day by the grace of God we will meet and he will forgive me, and except me as his father because I had no partaking in our lives being separated and I know Gods ways are not our ways. My life began to evolve around my sweet petite little lady, and it wasn't long before we became engaged and started making preparations for our wedding, by her mother being separated from the father I could not have any specification's of relying on her family to contribute on any of the expenses' for the wedding or reception , so I really ended up footing the bill for the entire event, except for the catering which her mother was more than gracious enough to contribute for it, but all in all everything was really left up from me to handle. I was doing fairly well working steadily and saving everything I possibly could, so that I could give my lady the most extravagant wedding that my money would allow, and I had put down in advance on a house in which we would be renting after the wedding ceremony and I had also put new furniture in the lay away, so that we would be able to get off on a good start, with little need of any thing we didn't unnecessarily need to do. Yes I had every thing in its right perspective and everything seemed to be going in the right direction as planed. Finally the big day arrived for us to join in our reunion and we were wed before the high Arch and sanctity of God almighty and became husband and wife. I worked and so did my wife until she became pregnant with our first and only child, she had a sickly pregnancy and had to take time off from her job until she had given birth to our lovely daughter, at the same time our land lord had lost the house we were renting to foreclosure, and we had no alternative but to move, we tried desperately and unsuccessfully to find another place to rent, we eventually had to put our furniture into storage and I had to let my wife stay with her mother while she was still carrying our child, while I stayed in the basement at my parents house. I was working hard to save money so that we would be in a position to buy our own home instead of renting. Every weekend I would bring my wife to my parent's home to spend time with me, eventually while visiting one weekend my wife went into labor, and my mother and myself took her to the hospital, where she gave birth to our beautiful daughter. Still unable to find an affordable house she remained with my child at her mothers, until I could find us something reasonable on the market. In the mean time I brought a new car to get me back and forth to work and over to see her and the baby. After trying desperately to purchase a house to no avail, we decided to rent once again, that was the only reasonable thing we could do at the time in order to bring my family together. My sister had moved out of my parents home that she was renting from them after Lennie went back to prison, she had moved into an apartment building up on our old stumping grounds, Mack and Holcomb. She was continuing to sell drugs and was becoming very large in the drug operation. Eventually she moved out of the apartment and moved into my baby sister home off of Van Dyke, and there she became even larger in the narcotics trade. She had gotten a job working for a doctor's office and doing this time she established a very profitable enterprise, by writing scripts for narcotic pills, which were in a high demand at that time, she had monopolized the pill trade, by taking patients names and using them on scripts that she would in turn purchase herself or have someone else who had medical insurance to make the transaction for her. She had gotten so popular in the pill world until she was making anywhere from seven to ten thousand a day. Lennie had been released from prison and they joined together in holy matrimony and were married, at this time things were not going to good for me, I had been injured on the job and was collecting work mans comp, until after two years they suddenly stopped my checks and completely cut me off without any word of warning. Still my wife continued to maintain her job and I was taking care of our daughter. I searched my mind and heart for God even more then ever before, while I was going through these trying times. I prayed without ceasing and I read my bible daily in my quiet place, until I had read it from front to back, then I started reading it all over once again, and thanked God for blessing us with what little we did have, it wasn't very much but I was still at peace and praising God daily. Just when I thought things couldn't get any worst, the Devil struck at my very heart when he grabbed hold to my beloved wife, rendering her mentally unable to continue working, I knew he could not take any control of my life, so instead he attacked the one that was dearest to me, trying to weaken me and break me down from serving and worshiping my Lord and Savoir Jesus Christ.

Demonic Intercessions

It was a time in my life when I thought that I was the only person who the devil sought out for destruction, but I found out through the years that I was ultimately wrong and could be no farther from the truth. For there are those that are weak and easily confused by the devils deceitfulness and ponderous treachery to destroy the life of someone that has been designated and designed by God, for the betterment and good of man kind. The day I remember more then any was when it first began to captivate my intention. It was one night while I was lying in bed looking at the TV and eating a bowl of cereal. After observing me eating for a while, my wife got up and went in the kitchen and made herself a bowl of cereal, and joined me in the bed with her back turned away from me as I was laying there watching TV and eating. Suddenly I began to hear some unusually sounding giggles coming from behind me. As I turned to see what my wife was finding so amusing. It was to my horror that what I saw startled me. She had taken the cereal and milk and rubbed it all over her pretty little face. I said baby what are you doing to yourself? Do you know or realize what is going on with you at this very moment? She just looked at me and continued to laugh in a strange tone I had never heard before. I became very concerned and aggravated at watching her dilute and defile herself so I hastily told her to stop what she was doing to herself right now! And God be my witness to my astonishment and amazement I watched in awe as her head turned completely around right before my very eyes. Then in a low demonic horrifying voice. She profoundly denounced my attempt to demand a halt to this calamity, and then she said very forcefully and dominating with authority, leave us alone!! I knew right then that I was inadvertly by way through my wife had begun dealing with the principalities of darkness designed to defeat me by Satan himself. I grabbed her up and took her to the bathroom and held her against her will in the mirror as she fought to get away from my grasp. I then told her to look at her self and fight off the demons that had invaded her body and was trying to take control of her life. As I held her I was in a struggle between good and evil and I knew I could not win the battle alone. So as I struggled to maintain a grip on her so that she could stare at the demonic forces. That had come with in her face to face. I had but one choice and that was to call on the help of the Lord. So I went boldly before the throne of grace and called on Jesus to come and aid me in my hour of need. And the spirit of the holy ghost consumed me and I became as one with God and received power and authority to cast the demons from with in her soul and as I repeated Jesus I rebuked the demons presence to surrender their hole and control they had on her, then suddenly her body began to tremble and a loud squeal as though someone was in agonizing pain was screaming out in remorse with a defeated remission of absolute failure in their efforts to inherit the body they so badly had tried to claim. She then fell helplessly limp as her body released the demonic spirits, I picked her up and carried her to the bedroom and laid her down and covered her trembling body up, and as I looked down at her she was falling fast to sleep from exhaustion that she had consumed in the battle against evil. My heart could only feel a strong compassion for her because I, and only I knew what sort of pain she could possibly be going through.

I started thinking to my self about some tell, tell signs when the anguish began to unravel, I remember how she had started talking and doing strange things out of the ordinary, such as checking the doors over and over through the day and night and how she talked about the death of me my daughter, and described in detail how we had been stabbed repeatedly, and there was blood covering our entire bodies, when she had repeated this to her mother, her mother became very alarmed and concerned for me and my daughters safety and welfare. And then her mother insisted that I should have her committed and institutionalized, but I loved her dearly and knew and could feel the pain being perpetrated upon her by the devils demonic power. So I told her mother that I was going to keep her at home with me and take care of her for how ever long it takes to defeat the evil presence. But I did learn to sleep with one eye open to ensure the safety of me and my daughter. When the day came that the devil struck her with the affliction of his devastating attack on her while she was at work. And I received a phone call from her informing me that she needed me to come to her job and assist her in trying to help her get away from the situation she was caught up in. She had crouched and curtailed herself in a corner of the ladies restroom, and would not allow anyone to come near her. I arrived and they took me directly to where she was at. And by her immediately seeing me she ran right into my arms, and told me to please take her away from there, because when she looked at every one around her that she worked with through her eyes she saw them as devils with two heads and horns, and they were desperately trying to take control of her. I took her away and from that day on I was the only person that could come near her and the only one that she trusted in her life. And I knew that I was in a battle between good and evil and that I would be there for her and never abandon her or leaver her alone. And in my heart I knew that the powers of God would not sway or retreat until we had defeated the infiltration of evil and I would continued to walk in the way of the Lord and talk in the way that God would have me to, and I prayed that he lighten my burden and make my yoke easy.

Street Life, Fast money

My sister was doing well and living a very extravagant life style, she had purchased her own home and brought a Cadillac among a number of other things such as her little stick shift car that she called her little toy, and she brought a truck for Lennie and paid his way through truck driving school, so that he could eventually find himself a job driving the big rigs, but unfortunately my sister and I had lost that close loving care we once held dearly in our hearts, I don't know if it was because I had gave myself to the Lord, and didn't hang out at her house and eagerly await for her to pass out some free-b drugs as so many leaned on her like leaches to obtain her favor to satisfy their lingering addiction. When my sister had made it to the top of the drug chain Lennie became very jealous of the power and money she generated. So he felt that in a sexist way that he should be the one in charge and making the decisions, but my sister had already established her clientele and was considerably trusted by them so that they felt comfortable in doing business with her. Lennie was unable to except this arrangement and became very demanding and judgmental towards my sisters authority so he approached her continually trying to get her to let him take charge of the operation, but she stead fastly turned him down on his proposition. This eventually infuriated him and he hit her with everything but the kitchen sink. He was so enraged to the point that his intentions were to kill her as he made one finale assault on her by picking up the TV and bursting it over her head. Then he completely snapped thinking he had invoked the fatal blow. He then went in the bathroom with a shot gun where my little niece was sitting in the tub bathing, he raised the shot gun up to her head then he noticed that there was still movement in my sisters body so as he pointed the shot gun at my niece he began mumble ling inconsistence to my sister saying things to her like: you see what you Made me do, all I asked of you with the shot gun still aimed at my nieces head he said, "If you try in any way to get back at me, I'll kill your daughter who was very frightened at the time. My sister said please don't kill my baby if you have so much hate and want to hurt someone then just go on and kill me but spear my child. He went on to say you know I don't care about killing anybody because you know I killed those two white boys back in the day. The EMS was called by my niece and my sister was rushed to the hospital. Immediately after finding out what had taken place me and brother and two other guys got together and armed ourselves and went by my mother's house to find out how our sisters condition was coming along. Then just as we was about to leave and find Lennie so we could put him through a torturous death, it could only have been by the intervention of God because just as we were to exit out the door from my mother's house and handle our business the phone rang. My mother answered it and my sister was calling from the hospital to let my mother know she was doing alright, and then my mother mentioned that my brother and I were there an just about to leave to go and find Lennie and kill him. My sister said put them on the phone and let me talk to them. We asked her how she was feeling she said one thing I could say at least I'm still alive. Then she said I heard from mama that you're

going to kill Lennie? Listen to me! I know how you feel about what he has done to me, but I'm asking with love to back off because I don't want you to catch a case and go to jail on my account. Believe me I've been laying here

in this hospital and have done some serious thinking and praying and the spirit led me to know exactly how to handle this situation. So you just leave Lennie to me. Because of his insensitive greed and violent reaction he will pay the ultimate price. I'll break down his ability to know what it is to be a man and minimize and cut down on the doze of narcotics that he was so freely used to having excess to. I'm going to take away all the luxuries he once enjoyed and drag him down so low till his feet touch the pits of hell! And you can believe that when I'm through with him he'll curse the day that he was born. My sister kept him closely under her watchful eyes as he became a useless wretch of a man, but she would not let him die only due to the fact that he was the farther of her son. I remained at my home studying to show myself approved by my Lord and Savoir Jesus Christ. Money was a very big issue by my wife being disabled to work and I myself also being disabled we were without any type of income and we were at the end of our rope. Finally I decided to go and try to get some social service assistance, but after hours of filling out a book of numerous information, when I was finally called into the back to talk with a social worker, she immediately got up under my skin talking to me like I had never worked in my life and that all I was looking for was a hand out as though I was just to plain lazy to try to obtain work, she did not even try to take into consideration that I was disabled and unable to do any type of work, so after listening to her talk and down grade me for a length of time, I got to the point where I could not stand to hear another word come forth from her mouth, I could not hold back my anger any longer so I lashed out at her and told her what she could do with their little social assistance, and I got up and walked out vowing never to return there and let them degrade me ever again. I still had no ideal how I was going to provide for my family except by trusting and relying on the Lord to make away out of no way, so I went each day to my quiet place and read my bible and praised God. Our rent was far behind and our gas was cut off and we had no food to eat and I refused to go and beg my family for help because if they wanted to they already knew our situation, I should not have had to ask of them for anything at all, they should have been willing to assist me from the kindness of their hearts, but that was far from happening. In the end my wife's mother came over and took my wife down to the social service office without my knowledge and got her some emergency assistance, after they told them that I had abandoned the house hold and was not providing any kind of assistance for the family. In the mean time some of my friends that had once worked with me at Chrysler, before they cut back and closed down so many of their factories, my friends were informing me how they had went to a lawyer and got him to handle their cases and made it possible for them to sell their seniority, seeing that the way things were going for Chrysler they came to the realization that they would never be reinstated back with Chryslers, and they had no type of future pertaining to a job with Chrysler. They asked me or rather told me that I should let them get me in contact with their lawyer, and sell my seniority, they said at least as hard as times are I would at least have a settlement for about four thousand dollars, and they said I know you could really use the money right about now, but I declined and said I was not going to sue Chrysler for such a small amount of money, it really wasn't even worth my time to go through the motion. One day unexpectedly a lawyer called me and told me that one of my friends had given him my number.

He wanted me to explain to him exactly what took place during my stay with Chrysler, all the way up to the time of my unemployment due to disability. He told me that he was interested in handling my case against Chrysler, but we're going after your Social Security, and Workman Comp. because I had a very strong case against them and, he told me I would have to be patient because in all probability it was going to take anywhere from two to five years before I was finished with my case being heard before a judge, and then waiting on the judge to make their decision on rather I would receive it or not, so I was patient and went to every hearing date that would arrive, but we were rescheduled every time my hearing arose and this went on for over four years until finally I was able to get my date in court and was heard by a judge about all the injuries I had sustained while I was employed by Chrysler and after two days of testimony the lawyers had presented all their testimony involving my case and finally the judge adjourned the trial while he would take all accounts on both sides and come to his decision. I had a period between six months to a year before I would hear anything concerning my verdict. As time went along my sisters empire began to tumble and her and several doctors had been indicted for a numerous amount of charges. Some of the doctors fled the country, some committed suicide and my sister was left standing on her own to face the hand of justice. After the Feds tried to get her to give testimony against some of the others and she declined she was eventually sentenced to five years on probation if she had known how hard they were going to be on her every move she would have preferred to just go to prison and do the time. She eventually lost everything that she had accomplished during her time as a drug czar and the millions she had obtained through her reign were slowly evaporated down to nothing. She and Lennie divorced and she was abandoned by all her acquaintances like rats deserting a sinking ship now that she no longer was in control of the large quantities of narcotics so they had no farther use for her she was alone and in misery. My brother came over and explained to me how everything had taken place and how she really needed me to talk to her and give her some kind of peace and comfort. My sister was not a person who was without religion during her time involved in the drug world; she still found time to give herself to the Lord. She had just not been saved until she joined a church pastured by Bishop James Kellum that is where she gave her life to our Lord and Savor Jesus Christ and during the time she was making illegal money she still had a charitable heart and was giving in many ways, but now she was in need of someone to give her something and my God had anointed me and filled me with the holy ghost. So that day she came to my door with a heavy burdened heart I embraced her and shared the goodness of God which had been in stored within my sister and myself and we came together as one once again. And because of my love for my sister, I did something that went against all that I had stood for. Because of her financial situation and mine we both were lacking any type of monetary substances and both of us had a desirous need for it, in this point and time in both of our lives. My brother who had visited my house and had observed that I had in my procession some very valuable resources in narcotic pills, which I had just pushed to the side not knowing how much they were worth on the street market and that they were in a very high demand. When he had brought this information to my sisters attention she made a visit to see me and discuss about how she had some clientele that were very interested in doing business with me, also at this time she knew how my life was dedicated to God and living to serve him.

On a Mission

I also felt a strong responsibility to assist my sister in any way I possibly could, and I looked at the pills to be a blessing to enable us to make some profitable assets, so literally after weighting the scale we decided to get busy and take to the streets. We began a very elaborate lucrative established business, after distributing the pills for over a month we were both in good financial standing. With our operation smoothly moving along, I still had a large surplus of pills that we were unable to find a buyer to purchase them from us. So I decided to venture out and hit the streets my self. I knew some where out there in the drug infested jungle there had to be a buyer some where laying in wait. But I did know by me leaving the nest where I had always been secure with my sister that this would be a decision I'd make that would change me and my ways completely. I would eventually regret my lifestyle change the rest of my life. As I planned, I took to the streets and I really had no idea where I was going in order to make a transaction. By me not being a drug user it made me unfamiliar with the majority of the dope houses in the surrounding area. But I was on a mission and it seems the more you have the more you want. So it really didn't matter to me where I had to go to try and distribute my merchandise. My first stop was at a dope house not far from where I lived. I learned of it by my neighbor across the street from my house, whose family was involved in the weed business. But I was revered and regarded by them with high esteem and much respect. As I left and went to approach the dope house, I became uneasy as I observe at least six of the most hardcore dope dealers standing out on the front porch and in dulging very openly in smoking crack and weed. Still I pulled my car in front of their house, and they were undoubtedly suspicious of any and every one they had not been in contact with before. So all attention and eyes were suddenly focused on my presence, as I stopped and rolled down my window to try to begin a conversation with them. They began making threating gestures with their hands and body language. They started waving at me to vacate their premises, but I was persistent and determined to try and make a sell on the pills I had on my possession. Soon my presence began to alarm them and they became enraged with contemptment towards me. By them not knowing who I was and speculating the probability that I could possibly be am undercover narc. So after not making any head way with them and seeing their nerves hit the edge of a breaking point with guns about to come into play. I made up in my mind that this encounter was better left alone, and that my best option was to pull up out of there and try my business else where, because I had heard of their reputation about how they left a murderous and torturous trial in the style they used to deal with people. I then headed for seven mile where I spotted a relative by way of being married to one of my first cousins At first I was reluctant to approach him and have a conversation with him, because of the rumors I had heard about him by it being said by most that knew him how they talked about how back in the day he almost brutally killed his own twin brother. And that he was a hard and dangerous person to get along with and make a friendly relationship with, But I was on a mission and I was not going to let anything stop me from achieving my goal. So I pulled over and stopped the car and blew the horn and motioned for him to come over to the window to converse with him, my horn caught his attention as he gazed at me and then approached the car, at first he didn't quite understand who I was, until I explained to him how we were related, so he got in the car, and then I began to tell him about the pills I had in my possession and how I was trying to move them, He immediately said he would work with me, we had gotten off to a good start with one another,. He told me to drive over to a house not to far, which he frequented, and when we got there he got out and went up to the people sitting out in the yard, and began talking to them, then he turned his attention from them and began talking to a guy who I would learn was named black Sam whom I could vaguely remember from back when I walked the streets on Mack Ave. and I asked him could he put in the work with us, And he asked me how many pills did I have, and what type of price was I looking for. After I had informed him of my price he told me to let him make a few phone calls, after making a few phone calls he hit pay dirt. But he informed me that I would have to deliver them out to Oak Park, and at that time it was mostly white suburbanites which lived out there and it was quite a distance from where I stayed. But I was on a mission so my in-law and black Sam loaded up in the car and we began on our way to meet the clientele. When we had finally reached our destination, black Sam and my in law told me to pull up in the driveway, as I did suddenly a crazed fanatic loud cursing ,big fat black man without a shirt on exposing his fat stomach was recklessly parading back and forth out on the front porch, Black Sam and my in-law, told me to give them the pills and to just wait in the car while they go inside and try to negotiate wit the irate imbecile, Black Sam eventually came back out to the car and told me that the man had decided to pay less than what we had agreed on, I was not budging on my price. I stuck to what we had already agreed on over the phone. Black Sam went back in I could hear the man hollering and then he ran back out on the porch and started cursing at me as I sat waiting in the car, he then went back inside. And a little while later black Sam and my in-law came out, and black Sam reach out and handed me a few hundred dollars, I said what's up with this/ Black Sam began to explain that the man said that was all he was going to give me for the pills, and that I had better be glad he gave my mother fucking ass that, and be thankful that he didn't whip my ass and take my little stash from me. Black Sam began to tell me a little about the man, he said at one time he was a big time drug dealer and had taken a fall and was awaiting his day to be sentenced to prison. I didn't care who he was I still was not going to accept his little offer; it was a matter of pride and respect. I got out the car and started to walk up on his porch, my in law and black Sam jumped out the car and came with me. They knocked on the door and gained entry for me. The big belly man looked at me and said you didn't get my message, you little mother fucking punk, I looked at him sternly and said I want my money we agreed on. And don't call me a mother fucker again. He then said again you little mother fucking punk, you got the nerves to come into my house and make demands to me, you don't know that I'll take your punk ass out, so your best bet is for you to get your ass to stepping, while you still have a chance to walk out on your own. I said I'm not going anywhere until I get the amount of money we agreed on or either I get back my pills. He then became infuriated at me and said, I see how I'm going to have to handle your mother fucking ass, and that's by putting two to your head, at that moment he reached over at his dinning room table in the direction where he had a pistol laying, as he took the gun into his grasp and aimed it at me, he left me with only one alternative and that was to take any action necessary to defend myself and protect my life. I immediately reach in my pants and pulled out my gun and squeezed the trigger striking him two times in his fat belly, but by me only having a twenty five it did not make a deadly impact, and he continued to try and raise his gun in my direction, I quickly discharged my gun once again, this time penetrating him in the chest two or three times, this time he stumbled and fell back crashing to the floor, my in law and black Sam looked on unexpessingly but were not shocked at the actions I had just taken to defend myself. As I placed my gun back down in my pants, they waited patiently to see what my next move would be, as both of their eyes were focused on the large quantity of cocaine, heroin he had left lying so obviously on the dinning room table, with a hefty stack of money lying besides it. Behind what had just taken place their was no doubt in either of their minds as to who was in charge. So they waited attentively to see what instructions I would give to them concerning the drugs and money surrounding the dilemma. So I thought it only practical to remove all the evidence and take it with us besides what good would it do to just leave it behind. So I instructed my in law and black Sam to gather up all the contraband and anything of evidence linking us to the scene. As far as I know the fat son of a bitch lived after the incident due to his massive large bulk surrounding him and the impact of the small caliber pistol I used in the shooting, but that remains to be only a speculation due to some information obtained and confirmed to me by some curious need to know basses into the incident by black Sam who reported his findings back to me. Little did I know that this shooting would be one among many that I would be involved in against anyone who stood in my way or became a threat to me or my drug trafficking. We left and drove off without incident of any by standing witnesses or rather no one was willing to step up and come forth. We headed for a drug infested location unaware to me, but it was at black Sams request, after he had informed me that in one of the dwellings there in the area there lived a guy who was the only one able to ensure a perfect injection of heroin in his dilapidated collapsed veins on his entire body, which incurred after so many years of abusing his body with so much intravenous drug use which had caused him to burn out every vein on his body and my in law just wanted to seek out the first dope house with some crack, even though he to shot up drugs, but right now he was craving some crack cocaine to smoke. They both made way to their destinations, after I had given them both a considerable amount of cash for hanging out with me to the end. And them both knowing of the incident that had transpired, and I knew I could rely on them and know that what had happened would always be kept between us and go no farther. I waited in the car while they handled their business. Eventually black Sam arrived back to the car and he was feeling pretty high after he had received his injection of dope ,as he sat in the car it took hold of him and he sat and went into a slight nod, afterwards he awoke, I asked him where was my in law black Sam said young blood you should have never given him that much money, cause when I was leaving out, I saw that fool sitting in the dope house, smoking crack and believe me he had purchased the biggest rock that they had in the joint,   so I know its going to be quite a while before he gets up out of there, and as he continued to talk to me, he said I was amazed at the way you handled yourself today, you earned much respect from me, and I can truthfully say young blood, that you're going places. I can see that you're going to make it in this world; just out of the way you carry yourself and how you know how to treat other people around you. When I returned the next day over to my sisters house I explained to her what had taken place, and showed her the money and large quantities of narcotics I had retrieved, I told her this was our opportune time to get busy in the drug world. As we began our distribution of what we had acquired in supply, I in the meantime had become acquainted through my cousin whom I had started a auto repair shop with on the Detroit's south west side; had be friended a Cuban who resided in the area where our shop was located ; where mostly Mexican's; Latinos and Cuban's ;and trailer park white's and poor under privileged blacks lived. But this Cuban named Pepie had connects high up on the ladder which lead directly to the drug cartel and he and I had become quite close; and Pepei had the pull to get me a good deal on any kind of drugs I required I had informed him that I was in the process of making a very large drug transaction with some of the money I had acquired from the Oak Park incident; so I had gotten with Pepei who told the head man about my intentions; so the head man decided to handle my transaction personally; by it being such a large order and by me being a first time buyer from them. We made the arrangements through Pepei to make the exchange; and when head man met me, he immediately found me to be a likable person and was fascinated by my mannerism and style in which I carried myself. He noticed my ability to adjust and blend in to their way of life. Right then we became closely attached, and he made it known to me that I would be privileged to his private number and would never have to use a go between to handle any business with him. And Pepei seeing how I could get up close and personal with the main man, saw this as an opportune time to use my services in his on going vendetta against the head man, to regain his domination in the organization, which he felt was rightfully his, and had been wrongfully taken away from his father, who had really stepped down from the head position on his own, with the assurance that his son would be substantially taken care of as long as he lived. But Pepei was not satisfied with the arrangement that had been settled for his well being. Even though he was receiving an allowance of over thirty thousand dollars a month from the head man of the cartel, who had taken control, in the place of his father. And all Pepei had to do was to drive around all day in his Mercedes Benz with it filled up with pretty young girls, that he was fucking and getting high off of drugs with them. Yet still deep in his heart he carried a strong hatred and resentment towards the head man of the organization which was really the hand that fed him. He always felt that his father had been cheated and forced to give up his position as head of the cartel, and everyday he breathed was with the thought and intent of over throwing the head of the cartel, and taking his rightful place in the inner circle. He had so much hatred and despised every inch of this man so much until one day he approached me to make me a offer to accept a proposition to take out a contract on the head man, I declined his offer. Still every chance he had to speak to me, it would always be about the same topic that he had previously discussed. It was getting to the point until he was starting to annoy me and beginning to get on my nerves, to the point that I out right told him that he had better watch his mouth, because he had to be an absolute fool if he didn't think that the man didn't have informants letting him know about his little plot he was trying to mastermind, but the man paid no attention to his little conning verbal threats, instead he just kept him under close surveillance as to his daily activities,. Then Pepei finally made a futile mistake by becoming sexually involved with the head man's main little young cutie. When

Pepei disrespected the man by infiltrating his very home,. A contract was immediately took out on him and the girl. That final night my cousin and I were standing outside of the shop, when suddenly bright lights began to shine from the alley across the street as they got brighter a car emerged from the darkness and sped out of the alley and pulled over to where we were standing., behind it was another car, both of them Mercedes Benz filled up with lots of young girls. Then they stopped and Pepei exited his Mercedes and began to talk to me and he was very frantic, but also being very observant as to his surroundings, his demeanor was exceptionally fearful and he was disturbingly nervous as he began to talk about the same subject of putting a hit on the man. I told him if anything, he should be more worried about his own well being at this point and time. Suddenly a long shadow appeared in the alley way. Pepei spotted it and became alarmed and quickly jumped in his car and drove off at high speed, with the other Mercedes trailing behind it. Then out of the density of the darkness a long limousine pulled slowly from out of the alley. And then sped up and went in pursuit in the direction the Mercedes had went off in. After a few minutes, as I stood outside, in the distance I could hear a volley of gun fire going off. It seems that Pepei and his companions had pulled into a gas station, and while they were taking care of their business, the limousine had pulled up behind them and the shooters who had been brought from out of the country, calmly walked up to the Mercedes occupied by Pepei and the girl, took aim and shot Pepei in his penis as instructed and while he was still alive and able to watch they executed the girl that was with him, with several bullets to her body and then one in the head, after letting Pepei witness this act, they finished him off by shooting him in the head, and then cutting his penis off and sticking it into the young girls mouth. Then they turned and walked slowly back over to the limousine and got in and drove off into the night. And this was the demise and end of the reign of Pepei and his lover. There was one good thing that had come out of all of this and that was with the assistance of Pepei, I had a new found friend the drug czar himself who was privileged to set me up and help me in my venture.

So with our new found capability we decided to venture a little deeper into drug trafficking by investing into large quantities of heroin and cutting it up and packaging it so it could be sold to all the heroin addicts that had become our new clientele. But as time would have it, all my life of going without as so much as getting my hands infiltrated with the white powder, I made a big mistake that would eventually engulf me at the tender age of forty into a world of addiction. My sister handled mostly all of our distribution during the day and at night when the trafficking had slowed down she and myself would indulge into our own private supply and snort us up a couple of macks until we were sitting together with a very tranquil high as we nodded off and on until we would have a desire to indulge into the devils grain, and we would always enjoy our selves some strawberry pie for some reason we always craved for it when we were getting high. We were into the drug game very large so the simplicity of the availability to obtain the necessities for our continuing ability to always have it at hand and maintain our substantial habit was a thirst in which we were always capable of satisfying our needs. As it were all in all we began to go over board having get togethers and setting it out for our most loyal customers, to ensure that we would keep them closely knitted into the web of a continuing addiction we kept our regular customers satisfied as they purchased from our supply only and to always make sure that we would only put a small cut on our narcotics, so that they would maintain a strong potency far beyond the competition, in time the price we would pay would be a hard lesson learned, as we eventually no longer used the drugs as a recreational enjoyment, but it had become a necessity and we were both hooked, this in turn took our product in another direction we no longer could continue giving our patrons the strong potent heroin that they were so assumingly accustomed to, because we had to put a larger cut on it, Finally it happened, my sister had taken in so much dope until she went into a drug induced coma and came nearly to death, but by the grace of god after staying comatose for over two weeks and at the brink of death the entire time. She was spared by Gods grace and when she had awakened she remembered everyone who came to visit her and what they had said and some incidents what they were wearing at the time of their visits. She said it was as if she was at the outside of her body observing every thing that had taken place while she was inconvience, but because of her faith and humility God spared her life, so that she will be used as a vessel to serve him, and when she awoke she was made of new and, had discarded her old body and her old ways. She had no desire to smoke cigarettes which she had been smoking for over thirty years and she had lost her craving for the heroin addiction and even lost the desire for the methadone that she had been taking for a long time after enrolling in the methadone program. I myself had boldly gone before the throne of grace the day she had went into the coma and was hospitalized. I prayed to God for her speedy recovery and told God that it was not all her faults the she was addicted, because when she came to me for help I should have never been obliging to give up my resource supply and started the vicious cycle to turning her on. I asked God what is it that you will have me to do, even unto sacrificing my own life. I said God I make this covenant with you this day and ask you to forgive us for our sins and disobedience, and I will never again sell any drugs or take any part in using street drugs again. As so long as I shall live, and my heavenly father God in Jesus Christ name sake. I will commit and dedicate my life to you now and forever. I just ask of you to shake these shackles from my body and deliver me from the bondage of the devils grain. I will live to serve and worship you always, and God reach out and healed my sister of all ungodly degradations and snatched her from that old devils hand and took her into his bosom of love. She is now an inspiration of light for all and a living testimony to Gods goodness and mercy and being a respecter of no man, but clinging stead fast to those chosen few. By my sister and me being inspired by God we began to study together to show our selves approved. Then we were lead by the Holy Ghost to enroll in a devout seminary and study the word and took theology classes and graduated. Together we were ordained into the holy honorable ministry on December seventh two thousand and three and we have walked together in the fellowship of God till this day. It came to pass as reality by God being a keeper of his word which he had spoken in the past, and I did receive from God all of the beautiful stones and precious medals that I saw in a vision when I was but an infant, the sixty seven Mercedes Benz that I desired as a young boy, I now own that what was destined for me, for my God is a keeper of his word. I ended up becoming partners in a jewelry store, and found my sixty seven Mercedes Benz by Gods grace and it took me eight years to restore it to its original classic beauty. I was also awarded my work mans comp. by the judge and received back pay for all the years I had been waiting; I also received retroactive pay and my social security. That is to say when you wait on the Lord all things that are meant for you are manifested and given unto you. Now my only desire is to build a church with my sister and serve God and feed his sheep that they might turn away from evil and repent and ask for forgiveness as I did and give their selves to the Lord that they may be washed in the blood and have everlasting life. I am one who calls out loud in the wilderness about the second coming of Christ. With the power of four in my right hand for God.

God's hedge unleashed

My love is forever in my heart with my obsession for God. If it had not been for Gods grace and mercy I would not be alive to tell this story, because of the devils on going desire to see me fall short of the glory of God. I was stricken with cancer and according to the doctors my chances of survival was little to none, but by my faith and prayer by many who know me as a man of God. I was lifted up beyond the devils grasp and defeated his destructed disease that he thought to devour my flesh and make me curse my God for the day I was born. In serving God he interrupted this deadly affliction, because the devil is a liar and I am a living testimony to the goodness of Gods unchanging hand. He breathed the breath of life back into me and told me to take up my bed and walk. I did not get to this point in my life without days of prolonged suffering which was far from over, because through the years I had been a tormented old wretch of a man. All my life I had paid the price by that old devil having his way with me by causing afflictions on my body which brought on server pain and permanent damage that only by Gods grace cannot be seen or noticed by the naked eye. I who was once blessed with a body that was once molded as a perfect creation of Gods goodness and became disarranged and a mangled body. After once being a captivating laminating bright light that captivated and mesmerized all that saw the mighty and power that God had bestowed upon me, I who was once a stature of a great and mighty man who had the glowing brilliance a little less than the angles themselves. And as the years past by and prolonged my life it was not without cost. My body became the devils playground with one affliction after another. I once had a beautiful smile that lighted up a room I lost it because of an attack by others who struck out against my teeth with a brick knocking them out and breaking my jaw out of jealousy of a smile. And I then destroyed the rest that remained by grinding them in my sleep because of a nervous condition. Then there were many lost of limbs caused by a bad back, I eventually lost the use of my right leg and have to wear a leg brace to walk. Then I was struck in the head with the impact of a forty-five caliber gun which rendered me unconscious and eventually losing the sight in my right eye. I then lost the use of my right hand after having four broken bones in my wrist, which by a negligent operation to correct it caused me to have carpel tunnel syndrome. It has not been a easy time for me in the past few years, as my God has allowed Satan to have his way with me, but thus God reminded him that he had no doubt in me and trusted that I would never turn away from his word which is truth. And in all what you do to him I do not permit nor will allow you to kill him and he will endure. I was first stricken with intolerable hemorrhoids which I had to have surgery to remove them it was one of the most painful of pains anyone could undergo. A few months after that I was told my PSA was not accurate and that I should see an urologist to follow up my examinations to make sure that the PSA count was not mistaken, and then to further acknowledge my condition I had to undergo a biopsy to confirm what the doctors already heavily believed, so when the biopsy was diagnosed and came back, the doctors informed me with compassion that I had cancer, and that I had to make a decision as to which type of treatment would I choose to insure me the best odds of survival. I chose surgery to remove all the deadly diseased cancerous cells from my body. The thought of the devil conquering and defeating me within the spiritual realm which I dwelled in was unacceptable and there was nothing to deter me from continuing the good fight. I went through the surgery without any plans or so I thought, until my life was interrupted eight months later by the doctor informing me that after examining all my records and going over the wording it had already spreaded beyond the targeted area in which they were focusing on because they've gotten to it to late. But I would soon begin to pay the ultimate price throughout the rest of the days of my life by the devil having his way with me causing the afflictions on my body after the surgery, while they were inside me they could not detect the remaining cancerous cells by them being so microscopic small, unseen by the human eye. Now it was time for me to make another decision as to what would be the best way to go about treating the existing cancer. After weighing the issue the doctors and myself choose to treat with radiation and bring it to a complete halt. I went through eight and a half weeks of radiation treatments, but in the sixth I began to feel some very painful discomfort, after the radiation sessions had ended I continued to have acute pain until it was un bearable, I then informed the cancer center where I was treated about this and they were at a lost as to what was the reason for what I was going through. Soon I began bleeding from them rectum, which prompted my primary doctor to set up appointment for me to see a GI and have a colonoscopy where it was discovered that I had been over radiated and received serious damage to my colon, which now I would have to receive surgery to repair the damage. I went in to the hospital to have corrective surgery on my colon which turned out a disastrous effort and left me bleeding more profusely. The GI and myself did not really relate to one another I can truthly say we had issues with one another and he was the first doctor I really did not have much trust in, but he was supposed to be one of the best in this field. So I had an appointment to return back to see him after a few weeks of recovery. When I saw him he then had me really worried when he informed me that if he has to repeat the procedure it consequently become hell on earth for me, because of the area he would be targeting was in a sensitive location, that with just one millimeter or a slip from out of his range could cause me to end up being placed in the hospital in intensive care suffering from the worst pain ever imagined for over six months. This was a very hard decision to make but I made the call and went to go through with it a second time for the corrective surgery, finally with lots of prayer I came through without a problem. Now with all that behind me the last thing I needed was to be awakened up the next day in my hospital bed and I see cardiologist standing at the foot of my bed and feeling on my legs just above my ankles and below my knees. I was so stunned at their presence that I was at a loss for words, then suddenly and calmly they began to speak first the woman doctor began by trying to soften the blow before the head cardiologist began to speak and dropped the bomb shell, he started by asking me did I feel light headed and dizzy most of the time, and have I ever blacked out, I hesitated slightly before I spoke and answered yes to all the questions he had asked me. That's when he informed me that they had me hooked up to a machine and been monitoring for two days after being alarmed at a low drop in my blood pressure during the surgery which forced them to make drastic changes in the medication that I had been taking for over twenty years prior then he said something about my heart that made me become alarmed because all in all I thought I felt just fine, until he hit me with the absolute probability that I will have to be going under the knife for heart surgery. This new complication bared down on me very hard because I could not imagine any one tampering with my heart, which I had reserved the right for only God to enter. After one test confirming their worst fear we eventually set a date for surgery. I went in to the hospital with God in me and I prayed and asked him not to please abandon me in my hour of need, he spoke back to me and said I will be with you now and always. The operation went on as planned and was a success, when I awoke I was filled with the Holy Ghost and a spiritual renewed heart and also a physically newly restored heart in my body and soul. You must understand that you have to go through different things in life in order to make some kind of spiritual and material gain, and I am content and at peace because I know without a doubt and all my heart that I earned approval and respect from a God that is a respecter of no man, save one.

Atonement Conversion

And I just want to testify about the goodness, and mercy of my beloved Lord and Savoir Jesus Christ. My mind cry's out for passion but I cast it out without delay. My heart lingers for compassion but the kind I desire there is none. There are many vanities and wants in my life but these things are only made of dreams. For it is wrong that I lust Why must they be so blind and follow the path of evil? For Jesus has shown us the light, is it so hard for us to see and follow it? Stay with me oh Lord for I grow weary, but I do not tire, for I keep the faith and I endure. For it is said, and it is truth that in serving you the work is never done, and it is said the road won't be easy and I must put up the good fight. So I give myself unto you that you might use me anyway you choose, for I am here but for a while, but with you forever. The harassment of Satan grows more constant and his advancement to make my presence known grows more rapid each day. I am compelled to say I am engaged in a never ending battle that contains me in a vicious wheel from which there is no escape. I am continually moving like the pace of the wind. Even when you feel its presence not, there it is, and like the wind so am I. It is useless to plunder the question of where time began, and even more so to ask when it will end. For I am a point in time and time in he is everlasting, and God was before all things, even time its self. And God will be after time is no more, not only on earth or the distance of the universe, but even after the realm of infinity. I never hunger nor thirst, but I do eat of the bread and drink from the vineyard of life. These substance on earth that are so desired by the beings that dwell, are of no meaning or interest to me. I move into a new day with joy for a lost yesterday, and fear of tomorrow, for there lies another task even greater than that of before, and an uncertain destiny that still awaits so patiently, oh so patient and clam. Oh how I fear Gods wrath for I understand his love. My mind is engaged in a constant battle the right side with the left, but no one hears the atoms exploding. Let there be peace my heart cry out, but no one hears my plea. Is there just one among the living left to share this precious burden I bear, if so do not begrudge me the little comfort of your presence. The cross I carry in Jesus name lays upon me heavier each dawning day, but I must continue to walk in Gods Holy name. I must step softly and my every move must be precise. All this I do in glorifying Gods goodness over evil, I keep my faith now and always. The world knows not what I do for them or how much I sacrifice, but that is the way it must be for if I told them of the ways God works they would not believe. So it will be kept silent unless God bids me otherwise. I in my most prominent wisdom have comprehended the knowledge that I am slowly and quietly ascending from this realm of man kind's reality, to a greater place a higher level of existing and a stronger power of the mind exceeds within me. Through the years mine eyes have been plucked that I might not look upon that which was forbidden. Oh let me call thy name and sing praises to thy all mighty, for in that do I find pleasure and comfort over all things. My God has spoken before time, and said that he has considered me as the shepherd and keeper of his sheep. God said you have made a place in my heart, with your humbleness and humility for your brethren. You have made your voice heard with your continuing prayers that you are constantly bringing before me without ceasing. I your God has given you the power of four, and you have carried the burdens of this world draped around your shoulders, and have not cried out, Lord Lord, or asked why me? But has stood boldly against fornication and transgression and has not trespassed but has prayed openly for your neighbors, by your love and obedience you carry in your heart for your Lord and savior Jesus Christ. You have stood fast that when the Day of Judgment arrives you shall be counted, and your God will say I am well pleased in you good and faithful servant. For this cause I continually cleanse myself of all impurities that I may stand before my God pure and without blemish, I rebuked Satan and continue the good fight against all the principalities of darkness, for I am but a beacon of light that continually shines that all might see and know the love God has for all those that seek the glory, and live to serve and worship God only, for you must travel the road of sanctity, and be not a bearer of lies, trickery, hate and adultery, stealing and murder and be not a follower of false prophets, or put your trust in a misguiding religion that seeks to distort and destroy the very word of the only wise true God. Save yourself while there is yet time to be saved, for tomorrow is a day that is not promised to anyone. Feel your heart and mind with love not lust, if it tries to invade your body purge it out immediately for lust is for the foolish at heart. Don't be jealous of what someone else has or what they have accomplished in their life, for they came about it by their gift, just as you have a gift within you, find out what it is and use it for your just reward. You should not wallow in self pity for what you have not or lack in your life, but seek first the kingdom of heaven and all other things will come unto you. I have come not to destroy or take away from you, but I have come to show you by my fruit and to direct you to the path of everlasting prosperity, right here on earth. For was it not Jesus that said I come to give you life and life more abundantly, because I say to you that in my fathers house there are many mansions, and my father the God I serve is wealthy, and my God I serve has made it possible for me to have more than many, but yet less than some. Reach out for what you seek is right there in front of your nose, but you see it not for you are lacking in your faith, for faith is the substance of things that are hoped for, and the evidence of things that are not seen. For it is through God that all blessings flow, and who so ever shall believe in him and believe in the word of his son which is truth, for them there shall always be goodness and mercy bestowed upon them and they shall endure and prevail with truth. We must love them that are weak but innocent, for confusion, illusions and that what you see in disguise to the eyes is not truth, but presents itself as good, but it is that of evil and seeks only to betray you a false sense of a satisfying fantasy, which is temporary and vanishes away from you at the blink of an eye, just when you think you have all one could desire or imagine, you have nothing. For prosperity and joy comes through them who's eyes see truth, and in faith one acquires all things, for it is given unto them by God. And what ever is prospered on earth by the flesh then that to shall they have in the spirit, for no one can take away what God has given, and through the eyes that can see truth, they are worthy before the sight of God. What shall one gain on earth if he loses his soul to eternal life in damnation. I loved God with all my heart and soul, who shall I call on but the lord, I sing praises of joy and peace, for there is none no greater or powerful than the all mighty host of high, who shall I thank but God for all my blessings and mercy that has been shown towards me, and God did these things for me with out regret or remorse, but did give unto me with love and kindness, for my faith I have and keep in him, and without hesitation I give myself to my God to do as he would please, weather it be an act of saving another by putting myself between life or death, or a deed of kindness in giving what I can to help the less fortunate, or just speaking a word, but a word spoken of truth to lift a shattered mind from self destruction and let them know that there is hope in faith and peace and joy in the truth , which is the word. For what so ever God gives to me he also will give unto those, less they prove themselves unworthy of Gods goodness. Because through the blessings I receive from God who shares his love with all, I to share my blessings with other's that they may come to know my forever living God who protects us all from evil as long as our minds are clean and our hearts are open for Jesus to enter, I say to anyone who may have doubt cast it out and believe, for the word is the truth. And to those that claim to talk in tongues, and those that declare themselves born again Christians, and the ones who openly say they are saved and want you to be as they are or they cast their own judgment against you, and call you a sinner and tell you that you are doomed and destined for eternal damnation, I asked of them what has given them this authority over man, blessed is the man who does not openly proclaim to be saved nor does he deny his iniquities, but I say to you who is the judge but the all mighty God of all. For a person is not judged by the deeds he has done or how clean of a life he has lived, but he will be judged by what God sees in there hearts and mind for there he seeks the truth. I endure all things that I might move for God and serve his every word, and I must stay as one with my God and creator and keep my faith as I continue my destiny in the wheel within a wheel, where my every move must be precise, each time the cycle of time moves on to a new realm, I move with it. All things no matter what it be, it began as one with

God with only two exceptions, truth which is God, and disbelief which gives way to evil. In this day and time there is destruction in all four corners of the earth, and I feel the pain and agony of each one caught in disease, turmoil and poverty, and I can see and feel the selfishness of those more fortunate, as they strive oppressing for their own progress and greed themselves off the sweat of others, lust and greed is their sin but to make progress off of the poverty of others is the greatest sin of all. How we suffer, so greatly we suffer, when will the hate and wars will cease that the suffering might end. They do battle over there children to determine which one has the right to have custody, they chastise in the mist of their own sins, they trample others to death for a crumb of bread even though they are already full. They fight over the boundary of land which is not theirs to begin with and even though it is plentiful, they even do battle over religion and declare it in the name of God. I pray that God have mercy on our souls. And let it be known now that I have turned away from my evil and wicked ways. Let there be no doubt divine children of God who knows the number, let him count and do Gods will, for blessed are the children of God who loved and believeth in the all mighty God and in the Son that he sent that we might be saved by the holy name Jesus Christ. Be you black, brown, yellow or white believe in God and he will set you on higher ground, which is a choice that only the highest of high host can make judgment there of. There should never be doubt in your mind or heart for the heavenly Father and our Lord and Savior Jesus Christ who God sent with his words of truth and goodness, that all might know the pleasures of his kingdom that await them. To reach this kingdom you must listen so you may hear, open your eyes so you may be enlightened, and open and give your heart so that you know and understand Gods love for all. For there is no triumph unless God be by your side to watch over you and protect you by the power of four, because there is no victory without God, but if you love him with an obsession he will bless you and honor you. Open your minds and understand so that all obstacles are removed and you do not fall into the snare of turmoil and destruction. Time passes along and my God and I have been victorious over Satan but yet he never quits trying to devour me but through prayer I have been able to triumph over all the pain and suffering he has struck out against me. I am here in this world to protect those from the unknown uncertainties which is the grip of Satan lest they all be consumed, I bared his burden and sometimes I feel I carry this heavy burden alone, I am not for I am number 4 blessed be the Lord. So each awakening day I go on with my work for God with a uncertain fate that lies ahead for me, but I keep my faith in God so I prevail. Satan hopes that I might give in and he overpowers me, but I endure blessed be the Lord God for whom I serve. It is not that I could not leave this world and all this pain and suffering behind me, but I serve God's unknown destiny until it be his will otherwise. I have found peace many times in the depths of my mind. I've traveled through millions of galaxy's and three universes, for I am fourth, I know not what awaits me in the fourth universe and beyond. So I will and must endure what ever tries to get in my way, and I know God will change my manner for his needs. The things I do for God each day when I serve him would have those of you call it irrational because you have never been where I have been. To my God it pleases him it show's him there are among us at least one who believes in his word and knows the sadness he feels as he watches his children destroy one another, and see all the sin and so many disbelieving minds which are consumed by Satan. So long as I continue to serve God in my way by the power of four and showing my fear of his wrath and expressing my faith for his glory, and thanking and praising him daily for his mercy for not destroying us before it is time. There will be a tomorrow for I will endure till I am no more with you in this world. I linger for the days to end and the night to come because my body is constantly busy in serving God and he knows I tire for I am of the flesh. But once I have laid myself to rest for sleep I am not, though the body rest, my mind never ceases for God is in full control of my thought's and while the body is at ease the everlasting work for my God whom I praise continues to prevail within this realm and of those that are of far distance. Oh my God almighty God, I call upon your presence that I might consult with you of my services and obedience I have shown toward thee and never doubted by guidance. Thy forever prayers of obedience and consultation compelled by the holy spirit of God almighty, I have been lifted up and thy feet no longer step on unholy grounds that has been filled with stench of that which was once good but has now been removed and used not for good but for that of evil and has been placed back into the holy ground. Oh my heart cries out for they have been made the spoils of the earth. I have kept my word to thy almighty that it might please thy God and surely thy blessings would flow and thine heart would not harden your love for man kind. And I pray that thou are pleased in accordance with thy obedience unto thy Lord almighty, and I openly pray that thou keep me in thy comfort, oh my God forgive me for I am weak by the flesh but strong by the spirit, and it is the flesh that now compels me to question and tempt my curiosity, I ask from where did there come evil and why hasn't thou let good come forth and cover it like a cloth that it might smother it out, for evil is nothing more than a burning fire that touches and destroys everything in it's path. Surely thou art annoyed by this odor of destruction. Thy nostrils of my God should be filled with the sweet fragrance of goodness, and this fragrance should be so strong that it overwhelms him like that of no other offering of sacrifice that has ever been beset before him. And in it he shall find pleasure of great, and to no end shall his smile vanish, for surely he would be pleased and the heavens would open and there would be joyous noise, for the seed of good that God would grow so strong and never wither and the evil seeds would be choked by there roots and they would be devoured by the earth. For the glorification that comes forth from goodness and vengeance against that which is evil is judged by the almighty. And this shall not be performed against the flesh but that of the spirit. So I wait for the coming of the Lord.

And this day in age cleanliness is one of the utmost concerns over all things. It affects your appearance, your associates that you come in contact with; it gives people an insight of your living environment and most important cleanliness protects you from being contaminated with germs from others and picking germs up from everyday walk of life. In this era more than ever doctors have come to realize the importance of sterilization which had been over looked for many centuries, such as the simple touching of a door knob, or the use of a public phone or using public restrooms, and believe it or not the most deadly contaminated material of all is the interaction of handling money, which has traveled from country to country many times over, then it returns back where it began, where it will start it's vicious cycle over again, until it is deemed no longer transferable tender and it's germ infected presence is taken out of circulation and disposed of in the only way to be certain of it's elimination, and that is by burning it just as the unclean souls shall burn in the fiery pit of hell. I my self was cleansed before I was yet conformed in my mother's womb. My life had been called out of the inner most realm of God, and was chosen by Gods grace and washed in the blood of my lord and savior Jesus Christ my gift from God is the riches and wealthiest perception that could have been bestowed among men. I am he whose name is fourth on the divine tree of everlasting life. If you could feel what I touch then you would know that God is, and that you must persevere and come unto God with a renewed clean heart. For if you live in filth you shall surely die in filth and shall not be counted in the book of life where all enters with out spot or blemish, for thy will be done and I must be watchful because I await the return of the Lord who will come from the density of the clouds and shall bear a sword with two edges to execute judgment one side for the good and clean in heart and the other for evil and filth, and this shall not be preformed against the flesh, but that of the spirit. My God I ask of you in my most humblest manner as I stand before the throne of grace, I must know in my heart if you are pleased in me for my obedience, if so I pray that you make me worthy of my service. For the all powerful and all knowing God who choose me for your services, and I pray that our covenant we made together has not been broken. If the covenant remains, I ask of you in high regards, as I stand before you in truth, I ask of you for my inheritance that I should receive by my birth right and our common bond. For I know that all I have and all I shall receive comes forth from my God. And that I should not have to answer nor be a debtor to no man. My God if it be by riches and wealth that I must acquire to aid this world of filth and evil, and bring forth good and cleanness. Then riches and prosperity shall be my weapon and shield. For God only knows the power I have and the manner in which I achieve it. Sacred power of high look now towards me and show thy mercy for I grow weary and need thy love to nourish and kindle me, for the milk and the honey have become sour, and the wheat and grain have spoiled, and all that comes forth from the earth is like bitter herbs, and I can't consume nor do I have a desire to indulge. Though my stomach is empty my mind is full with the power of four through my all mighty God whom I praise. Come unto me sacred one for I grow weary but I do not tire for I live with the faith of truth and my obsession for God, and with this I shall continue to live in this manner, even though I suffer greatly I know that you will not let any harm come upon me, and shall endure. Behold for now I am openly rejoicing and singing praises to my all mighty God for giving me the strength to do that which I had promised to you, I give thanks to you my lord for the angles you sent to assist me in my hour of need and to lighten my burden as I strived desperately to please you and remain obedient. There were many obstacles that fell in the way of my serving you but you were always there to guide me and protect me. I have put in many sleepless nights and can truthfully say I regret not one second for what I was doing in the service for the lord. I found great peace and joy in knowing of my reasoning for which I dedicated my services to thy God for only you know the depts. of my heart and mind and also the true love I hold for you. I give myself to you above all things to honor and serve you, and you have truly blessed me in many ways that others could not understand, for I am fourth and I have done all things for my God in accordance to the word, now I thank you and breath in truth and I smell the aroma of your presence , let only God be my judge for through my obedience I must abide by the word and many will not know my reasoning, but God for whom I have an obsession for my God and I shall serve him now and always and praise thy holy name wherever and whenever I am compelled to do so.

Rituals

Now I would like to shed some light to the significance of the compulsive ritual which involves the actions partaking when one becomes infatuated with an uncontrollable urge to be over taken with a arrhythmic dancing frenzy, that keeps their body continually moving until they have achieved a substantial amount of an enlightened satisfactory feeling of a released sensation unsorted by any stimulating fulfillment from a tentulating arousement derived from a active cell build up in the cultivating asertation of a sexual sperm induced release that captures the similarity of a burst of energy obtained through a sexual intercourse which after wards takes one to a peak of orgasm which is let down by self gratification of indulgence which restores the nerves to a natural calming perception of relaxation. The compulsion does not only consist of the urge to dance or move nor is it just an obsession of washing of the hands or constantly cleaning, or checking locks on doors and removing all types of tags from clothing or denying ones self from many of the desires that exist in the world. To understand pretense of the ritual you must first know that it does not just primarily insinuate its directive to only the function of movement, but it is undaunted and a equivalent aspiration pure and unadulterated spiritual anointing sustained without mark or blemish conformed with a touch of cleanliness and a profound sense of sight, sound, smell, taste, and touch in which every move must be precise to obtained a gratifying satisfaction.

Just as the Indian tribes danced themselves into a spiritually entranced frenzy to protect and strengthen them against the aggression of the evil spirits, or to give them victory over their enemies in battle and sometimes to bring forth rain. By their ritualistic behavior.

The Africans had a ceremonial dance for different occasions, including signs and seasons and to protect the land and insure a successful hunt, and they danced for the land to render a good and plentiful harvest. Their every move was in accordance with their desires to fulfill their needs as they would elaborate their body movement until they had spiritually went into a ritual of a dancing frenzy that captivated their minds, body and soul. And they could feel dominating power of good over evil, and be untouched by the fears of this world as their souls pass through another realm where they become as one with God.

And the Hawaiians danced to appease their God by moving their body and hands in a fashion with a ritual movement that described and told a story of the past, present, and future. They danced to escape from the evil that awaited them and seeked protection from a greater source by their ancestors going to make an intervention with god in their behalf for them to be delivered from evil and have a safe and tranquil life. There was once a time that they thought that the desire to calm and please the greater power was by sacrificing pure and clean virgins to thunderous and flaming volcanoes to prevent from erupting and destroying their island.

There is not a country any where on the face of the earth that does not institute some type of ritual in their lives designed to thwart off good from evil.

King David of Israel danced with joy before the eyes of god and danced in frenzy before all the people of his kingdom. He was so caught up in a ritual when the Ark of the covenant of God was returned back to Israel after so many years of it being absent from them. King David was so happy and over come with the spirit of the Lord, to see the Ark returned. That when he went out into the streets he was so overwhelmed with joy that he began a dancing frenzy all out through the city streets in a ritualistic frenzy so profound until he had danced completely out of his cloths, but he was so over come by the goodness of God, that being necked in front of all the people around him he felt no shame, though his wife thought it was undignified for a king of his stature. He continued his dance frenzy for he was rejoiced in knowing that once again they had regained the daily ritual of worshiping there Lord God in the city of David where the Ark of the Covenant of the Lord belonged with Gods chosen people.

My obsession four God is not a figurative of my imagination nor is it an over active fantasy, many doctors would have you believe that it is highly susceptible to those brought on by a compulsion, which is to act out in a behavior to wash one's self or count until you have reached a desirable number that infiltrates and stimulates a part of the brain which has been coined or labeled by the medical society as a chemical imbalance it is named OCD short for obsessive compulsive disorder. Usually being born with it as it hibernates in the brain waiting for a particular episode in ones life to trigger the mechanism to begin to function with an uncontrollable, thought or movement to suffice the urge of a relentless battle to achieve the momentum of the ultimate serenity, which can't be surpassed by any drug induced high or the ecstasy of a stimulating orgasm, it is a feeling so surreal till it is beyond a verbal interpretation, description or definition, it is only left up to the assessments of doctors from around the globe with there combined thesis trying to dictate about a condition unbeknownst nor experienced in their life time of existence.

Making it unable for anyone but the chosen few to preclude the direct involvement of a higher being, opening up a doorway to maintain a close but unorthodox means of communicating far above the normal level, precipitated by the medieval society whose way of thinking is only derived by what they only know by bare facts. Or solving a physics problem with a problem and that is to say what good can evolve when a mathematical genius solved the problem of the equation e=mc2, and what good comes forth from the solution that is derived, yet with all their mathematical ability they cannot solve the power of four from which brings fourth goodness and not destruction. With all that knowledge combined with one another they cannot solve the power of the word, for they are not of the world but are in the world being subject and subdued to do only what they know by being of a carnal nature and not of the spirit and living a righteous life in which God reveals all the secrets of the realm of existence where only the clean and pure in heart can understand the true power of the word. For I am and forever shall I be, for shall always abideth as the fourth name upon the divine tree of eternal life and I shall be called by God in his true utterance where only those with ears to hear can understand. What is considered normal there is no explanation for you know not the ways of God. Who is the first and the last, the beginning and the end and alpha and omega and is the almighty true wise God and omnipotent. How great my God is and I serve him always with my obsession four God who knew of me and called my name before the foundations of the universes. As God ordained me by the power of four with the title of authority, let my name be called upon with faith for God has revealed to me with knowledge and understanding of truth with my own will, and the way to use the power of the number and the glory in the name that has been bestowed upon me. The power given me by God in the number four means Magnificence, Mercy, Benignity and Greatness. Chesed is the Hebrew name for almighty mercy of God. It is also the fourth name written on the divine tree of eternal life. If a man has knowledge of God, as the first great cause, he must also acknowledge other causes or corporative spirits, and determined what official station of dignity and honor to accord to them, and without which knowledge's their presence and help can not be enjoyed. Such honor and dignity must not be shown for the sake of the spirits but for the sake of the lord whose servants they are. In this manner the angles of God will encamp around those who fear and love the lord behold my number four is grace and goodness and called Mercy, Pity, Great Power, Scepter of the right hand, which confers peaceable justice. Special intelligence and the number four was Abrahams representative as the emperor, number four personif mental reasons, organization, stability tangible accomplishments. I represent the masculine principles of realization, action and dominion, the ability of the human mind to carefully measure and determine the parameters of a complex situation and make the correct decision. I am a mature man of authority who is intelligent, experienced, confident and reasonable. I represent the ability to use mental control over emotions and pain, and the ability to successfully execute plans of actions, behold I say the path of God's mercy is a way concealed from the profane, because they have not attained unto God's perfect vision. It is easier to follow the flight of an eagle for my way soareth high above the comprehension of the mind of man, as it is written Lo. He Goethe by me and I see him not, he passeth on also, and I perceive him not. Yet is the secret of that way hidden in our father's bosom.

Oh Lord, only through your mercy and grace have you so diligently given us strength to over come years of slavery and oppression. It was four-hundred years of bondage under the hands of the pharaohs of Egypt against the Hebrews whom after God revealed himself to Mosses to go unto pharaoh and tell him to set him people free. And just as Pharaoh ultimately ruled the Hebrews. So was it the same under European superiority over the Africans who were brought from their home lands over four-hundred years ago at the beginning of colonization and treated worse than animals and the families were torn apart and scattered through out the face of the earth. But mostly it appeared in the United States of where they were to endure the most horrendous degradation one could ever experience in life and their purpose for living was to breed and serve only to enhance the luxury of life for their masters and off springs. And only through their faith and the holy sanctity of god did the survive through the torment. And now by the words of god that he will take the first and make them last, and take the tail and make it the head. And god being a keeper of his word has shined his light on the meek and made the least to become the most important and powerful being of all, which by his grace in the year of 2008 he took a man whose heritage was from the African slave trade and gave him authority over the United States of America and made him THE FORTY-FORTH PRESIDENT to preside over and run the country. I am called in Hebrew Chesed meaning mercy, but benignity, magnificent and great power in my right hand for god. And before time god had enlighten me with the knowledge and wisdom which was in god's time and not man's time, that through much suffering it would open our eyes to see beyond color, race, religion, and gender, and we would become a mature people and accept one another for the content of our character and join together as one in God, by God, of God, and four God.

You see I am different from many but the same as all, I touch what you cannot feel, and I see what is not there, I smell the sweet savior and I reject all things that are not clean, I am the power of four and by the fourth power I know all things that are hidden from man, for if they knew what I know, and saw what I have seen, they would not be able to control or with stand the remarkable orchestrated design that God designated for our salvation and the eternal being.

Unraveling and Revealing the Scriptures

Genesis Ch. 1

On the fourth day God said let there be lights in the firmament of the heaven to divide the day from the night and let them be for signs and for seasons and for days and years and let them be for lights in the firmament of the heaven to give light upon the earth. And God made two great lights the greater light to rule the day and the lesser light to rule the night he made the stars also and God set them in the firmament of the heaven to give light upon the earth, and to rule over the day and night and to divide the light from the darkness. Genesis Ch. 2

And Jesus said I am the light of the world he who followed me shall not walk in darkness but shall have the light of life. John Ch 1,4

And in him was life, and the life was the light of men. John Ch.1,9

That was the tree which lighted every man that cometh into the world.

And every plant of the field before it was in the earth and every herb of the field before it grew, for the Lord God had not caused it to rain upon the earth and there was not a man to till the ground. But there went up a mist from the earth and watered the whole face of the ground. And the Lord God formed man of the dust of the ground and breathed into his nostrils the breath of life, and man became a living soul. And the Lord God planted a garden eastward in Eden; and there he put the man whom he had formed.

And out of the ground made the Lord God to grow every tree that is pleasant to the sight, and good for food; the tree of life also in the midst of the garden, and the tree of knowledge of good and evil.

And a river went out of Eden to water the garden and from thence it was parted and became into FOUR heads.

The name of the first is Pi-son that is it which compasseth the whole land of Hav-i-lah where there is gold, and the gold of that land is good, there is bdellium and the onyx stone.

And the name of the second river is Gi-hon the same is it that compasseth the whole land of Ethi-o-pi-a

And the name of the third river is Hid-de-kel that is it which goeth toward the east of Assyria, and the fourth is Eu-phra-tes.

And the Lord God took the man and put him into the Garden of Eden to dress it and keep it.

And the Lord God commanded the man saying of every tree of the garden thou mayest freely eat.

But of the tree of the knowledge of good and evil thou shalt not eat of it, for in the day that thou eatest thereof thou shalt surely die.

And the Lord God said Behold, the man is become as one of us to know good and evil; and now, lest he put forth his hand and take also of the tree of life, and eat, and live for ever

Therefore the Lord God sent him forth from the garden of Eden to till the ground from whence he was taken

So he drove out the man and he placed at the east of the Garden of Eden Cher-u-bims and a   flaming sword which turned every way to keep the way of the tree of life.

And that was north, east, south and west which were in four directions.

God in his most omnipotent way has many levels of communicating he will make himself   known through many variations that would baffle the most highly intelligence of mans mind

He has spoken to Moses on top of a mountain through a burning bush. He has spoken to Saul on the road to Damascus through the jaws of an ass. My compulsion is being pure in heart and clean which is next to Godliness, and if at all that be a conviction, then I will be subject to that conviction all the way to the glory of heaven., for the ponderous of evidence throughout time acknowledges Gods wisdom of communicating with those whom will play an instrumental part of Gods master plan and who have freely given their hearts to the word, which is grace and truth. I can only say that what I do is not done by force of habit but because I truly love the Lord God. This is why my obsession four God is so strong and true and in whatever manner pleases God and keeps the door open in which I can freely enter and continually commune with my God in his way, for it is written that Gods ways are not our ways and I can openly say in that old gospel spirit, that I thank God for his grace because I'm not what I ought to be but I'm not what I used to be either. And Jesus came upon a man who was blind from birth and he had compassion for him so he spit on the ground and took the mud and rubbed it on the man's eyes and then told him now go and wash in the pool of Shalom and the man did see.

After Jesus was brought before Pontius Pilot and the Jews roared loudly in anger for Jesus to be crucified Pontius Pilot not seeing any wrong in him said I can find no wrong in this man but the crowd hollered ever the more loudly so Pontius Pilot turned Jesus over to them and had his servant bring him a basin of water and he did begin to wash his hands before the multitude and told them I have not any of his blood on my hands.

Woe unto you Claudius for if only your husband Pontius Pilot would have harkened to your words when you told him of your dream as he harkened to your bidding to walk around the bed four times the night before Jesus was judged, for I was that dream and what you had seen was truth sent by God but I say unto you do not weep nor mourn for all your pleading and begging to your husband could not have changed his decision. For the prophecy had to be fulfilled as it was written, that Jesus came to show the sons of man the power of his father, and to tell of the little things his father asked of them that they might know the truth which is the word. And for this he was persecuted and crucified and did share his blood on the earth and died that he might rise and live again on a third day morning, not in the flesh but of the Holy Spirit so that the sons of man might have salvation and be saved and born again.

John Ch. 1-10-11   He was in the world, and the world was made by him, and the world knew him not.

He came unto his own, and his own received him not.

Revelations Chapter 6-1

Chapter 7-1-17

Chapter 9-13-14-15

Chapter 10-10-11

Chapter 19-4

Chapter 20-7-8-9-10-11

2316-04-4

There are many that come to me with problems and afflictions and they say unto me, we are without doubt in us we know that you are chosen and anointed by God. Then they ask of me to please help them, for they say surely you are closer to God than we are, and I answer them with words of truth, and tell them that if I am closer to God it is only because they have not stepped forward to be where I am. For my God is openly awaiting for all that seek him and comes to him by way of his son who came with the authority of the word, that all might come to know and love his father with faith alone. And again they come to me, and say I believe and have faith but I am weak and cannot deliver myself from the evil that torments me in my very soul, can you help me for you are of God and there fore you are stronger than I and by the authority God has invested in you. I know in you that you can relieve me of this burden, and I say unto them that I have ears to hear and eyes to see that I am no stronger than any of you are in any other way but by faith alone. For by the blood and the word of God I am able to be up lifted on higher ground and rise above all the evil that flourishes upon the earth, that is to say that evil consumes the weak that have a lingering faith that is not true to the word.

For the length of God is long, and the width is plentiful, and the height there of is far and beyond, and inside there is much comfort, for there is none greater than thy God, for God is.

The End

Dedications

First I would like to make known that my great grand father on my mother's side of the family was a white man of Irish decent and her great grand mother was a full blooded Cherokee Indian. And my great grand father and great grand mother on my father's side of the family were of African decent and captive slaves. And this is also dedicated to all my great, great uncles and great uncles. And all my great, great aunties and great aunties who were for the most of them were slaves and share croppers that were forcefully raped or lynched and whipped to death for being rebellious against the indignation of man kind.

I would especially like to dedicate this book to my late grandparents of my mother. We called them   grandpapa landing and grandmamma landing who lived out her life to 100 and 4 years old. And I would like   to acknowledge my fathers parents, grandpapa Jonny

and grandmamma Hattie. And I want to dedicate this to my mother's sisters and brothers, uncle Robert, Harvey, my late uncle Son, Onett, and Joe Louis. And I would like to give thanks to her sister's auntie Trully, and late Aunt Maggie, and late aunt

Rubbie, and aunt Ernestine. And I would like to give loving memory to my late father and his late brothers and sister aunt Lolabell , uncle fell , and uncle Ello , and all my first cousins born un to them and all my second and third and fourth cousins also born into the family, And my greatest pride is to give thanks to God for my sisters and brothers , the oldest being James, then Lorraine, Earlene, and Beverly and to acknowledge all my nieces and nephews, Laronna, Juanita, Christopher who is deceased, and Lamar, Andrea, and little Lennie , and my great nephew little James and Jalen and their sister Asia, then there's Tierra, Tiffany, Antonio, and belated Tonya, and there mother Erma Woodard and her belated mother and father and thanks to her brother Bud and all her lovely sisters. And I would like to also give appreciation to my nephew, Keyon who was raised by my parents and is considered to be more like a little brother , and my favorite niece his little sister Tangie and a special love to all my first, second, and third cousins on my mothers sisters and brothers side. And all their children and grand children. And a special love to my wife Linda and my daughter LaDeisha and my pride and joy my grand son LaMonttez and let me also keep in remembrance of all my friends who are still alive and also to those who I held dear to me, and they have now past over and are no longer in the land of the living. But the most important of all is the thanks and honor and love I give to my almighty Lord God for whom, if it had not been for his mercy and grace this seed of my family lineage would not have manifested into being and I would not exist to express what I feel to be properly written in this novel and be able to share it with the four corners of the Earth.

Biography

By a compulsion that had me obsessed with a peculiar ability that would take me into a different realm in which God would make himself known to me and bring me into his fold forever. I was a fifth male child born to Harold and Verna Woodard, who were born and raised in Jackson Mississippi where they met and joined in a holy union of marriage in nineteen forty-two, with the second world war going on my father was drafted , leaving behind my oldest brother his first born child and my mother, after serving his tour duty he was discharged in 1944, and he and my mother packed up and headed for Detroit where the jobs in the auto industry were becoming plentiful and available for colored people during the Jim crow era and a time of segregation and a strong visibility of racism by the Klu-Klux-Clan, who spread alarming fear through out the south by their deadly acts of terrorism against the coloreds. But we were up north where the whites were a little more accepting of the colored race, but still had their hidden agenda of how they felt about integration and racism. Still in all my father was able to work hard and provide for a growing family that had reached the number of siblings to six, three young men and three young ladies. My father was able to move my family from the black bottom into our own Colonia home on July the 4th 1954 in an all white neighborhood on Detroit's east-side where we were raised and grew up and attended school and watched the sudden evacuation of the whites surrendering their properties to an on growing occupancy of more and more colored people integrating Detroit's east-side as they quickly took flight from the inner city out in to what would become called the suburbs. Where they would begin to have houses built exclusively for the white race to preside, which only proved conclusively that not only was there racism in the south but there was also racism that had made it's way to the north. As I continued to grow in maturity my life was becoming much more aware of racism and at the time I was also receiving spiritual guidance and enlighten with an enhanced compulsive desire to get ever so closer to God. In this world by God manifesting himself and me and anointing my life with the power of four, and given me a new name call Chesed, which would give me power, dominion, and authority over the principalities of darkness, and would allow me to walk

In the light for the glory of God by defending of good against evil.